Kindergartens

Educational Spaces

Kindergartens
Educational Spaces

Michelle Galindo

BRAUN

CONTENTS

6 Preface

Small: 150–1000 m²

12 Olifantsvlei Preschool
studio3 - Institute for Experimental Architecture

16 Kindergarten in Murcia
cercadelcielo. studio architecture

20 Les Petits Lardons Nursery
Agence Beckmann-N'Thépé Architectes

24 Arreletes Daycare Center
XVStudio

28 Kinderland Westside
raumhochrosen

32 Children in the Garden
Extension Kindergarten Rohrendorf / Krems
GABU Heindl Architektur

36 Svartlamoen Nursery
Brendeland & Kristoffersen

40 De Kleine Kikker
Drost + van Veen architecten

44 Taka-Tuka-Land
Susanne Hofmann Architekten. Baupiloten

48 Crèche in Arosio
Pietro Boschetti

52 Kindergarten Somereng and Fjellvegen
70°N Arkitektur

56 Company Nursery
Antonio Citterio Patricia Viel and Partners

60 Kindergarten Dandelion Clock
Ecker Architekten

64 Daycare Center and Municipal Dining
Hall Los Mondragones
Elisa Valero Ramos

68 Kindergarten Bizau
Bernardo Bader

72 Suruga Kindergarten
Taku Sakaushi + Chika Kijima / O.F.D.A.

76 Kindergarten Niederdorf,
Reconstruction & Extension
Stifter + Bachmann

80 Kindergarten Deutsch-Wagram
Architekturbüro Reinberg

84 Berçário Primetime
Marcio Kogan

88 Maison de la Petite Enfance St Saulve
Béal & Blanckaert architectes associés

90 Nursery School in Covolo di Pederobba
C + S Associati

94 Els Colors Kindergarten
RCR Aranda Pigem Vilalta arquitectes

Medium: 1000–1500 m²

100 Kindergarten Sighartstein
Kadawittfeldarchitektur

104 Kindergarten in Ramat Hasharon
Lev-Gargir Architects

108 Crèche Schwieberdingen
D'Inka Scheible Hoffmann Architekten BDA

112 Enterprise Crèche of the Metro Group
Marc Eller Architekten

116 **Daycare Center Skanderborggade**
Dorte Mandrup Arkitekter

120 **Space of Infantile Life of Carfagni-Chateaubriand**
MPH architectes

122 **Ajurinmäki Daycare Center**
AFKS Architects

126 **Crèche de Bernex**
Aeby & Perneger

130 **Kindergarten Neumarkt**
Schneider & Lengauer Architekten

134 **Maison de la Petite Enfance St Quentin**
Béal & Blanckaert architectes associés

138 **Fuji Kindergarten**
Takahuru+Yui Tezuka Architects

142 **Children's House Dragen**
C. F. Møller Architects

146 **Kindergarten Egg**
Dietrich Untertrifaller Architekten

150 **Crèche and Early Childhood Center**
Hamonic + Masson

154 **Kindergarten Barbapapà**
ccd studio

158 **Children's Day Home Schukowitzgasse**
Architekturbüro Reinberg

160 **Pupil's Crèche Kaysergarten**
Johannes Wiesflecker

164 **Structure of Receipt of the Small Infancy / Tonkinelle**
Bonnard Woeffray Architectes

168 **Oliver Kindergarten**
Hans Finner Architekt + Carroquino Arquitectos

172 **Nursery School in Marmoutier**
Dominique Coulon et associés

174 **Paletten**
CEBRA

178 **Kindergarten and Parking in Sansaburu**
VAUMM arquitectura & urbanismo

182 **Bubbletecture M**
Shuhei Endo

186 **Kindergarten in Sotillo de la Adrada**
BmasC Architects

188 **Machida Shizen-Kindergarten**
Akio Nakasa + Tomohiro Tanaka / naf architect & design

192 **La Corita Kindergarten**
Gálvez + Wieczorek arquitectura

//
Large: 1500+ m²
//

198 **Epinay Nursery School**
BP Architectures member of Collective PLAN 01

202 **Montessori School Landsmeer**
Rudy Uytenhaak Architectenbureau BV

206 **Nursery School in Pamplona**
Javier Larraz

210 **Las Viñas Infant Educational Center**
Solinas Verd Arquitectos

214 **Kindergarten in Rosales del Canal**
Magén Arquitectos

218 **Katarina Frankopan Kindergarten**
Randic Turato architects

222 **Saint Petri Parish Hall with Crèche**
Akyol Kamps Architekten

224 **Daycare Center for Benetton**
Alberto Campo Baeza

228 **Children's Day Nursery and Pre-School Hamm**
witry & witry architecture urbanisme

232 **Daycare Center Josefinum**
Nussmüller Architekten

234 **Kindergarten MB**
Njiric + Arhitekti

238 **De Uitkijck**
Bureau Bos

240 **Kindergarten and Nursery Jarun**
Penezic & Rogina Architects

244 **Oslo International School**
Jarmund/Vigsnæs AS Architects MNAL

248 **Copalita School and Civic Center**
128 Architecture & Urban Design

250 **Multifunctional Center Leeuwarden**
Rudy Uytenhaak Architectenbureau BV

252 **Forum 't Zand**
VenhoevenCS

256 **Primary School Daycare Center and Sports Hall**
4a Architekten

258 **Dietro la Vigna**
De8 architetti

Stimulating, creative environments for children.

by Michelle Galindo

Building for children, whether in the form of a nursery school, daycare center or kindergarten, certainly presents a special challenge for designers. What architectural language is suitable? How can one lend appropriate spatial form to a pedagogic concept that seeks to impart certain values and abilities? In an environment where young people come to experience and comprehend the world around them, every aspect plays a crucial role.

///

Focusing on the fundamental influence of sensory stimuli on a child's development, this volume presents around 70 outstanding, recent interpretations of 'meaning' in kindergarten design worldwide, each a successful rendering of the qualities that contribute to ideal spaces for children, combined with innovative architectural practices.

///

The design of this building type reflects the utopian ideals of its designers - that children should be encouraged to be creative, sensitive, imaginative, and original. The spaces inside the premises should encourage the children to ac-knowledge both their surroundings and their own body, explore various ways of playing and moving, interact socially with the other children, and develop their language and sensory capabilities.

Furthermore, along with stimulating a child's interest, they should provide spaces and facilities that are secure and safe, with materials that absorb noise, as well as the inevitable fall! The most important element of the design is the children themselves who provide the color, movement, sound and action; the quieter and calmer the surroundings, the more room for the kids' own creativity.

///

Practitioners of kindergarten design lower their spatial perspectives to meet the little clients' demanding needs and find new ways to work imaginatively within budget constraints. The spatial perception of the child is different; their point of view is considerably lower than that of the adult, and, raising their heads, they experience different perspectives that expand the relative size of objects. For instance, walls at odd heights, which may seem wrong to the eye of an adult observer, appear as normal to the children who give life to the building and with whom the building should ultimately communicate.

//

This volume features the work of well-known and emerging designers for whom design and play are entirely compatible. The creative design of the Kindergarten Taka-Tuka-Land in Berlin by Baupiloten was inspired by children playing; here, Pippi Longstocking's old oak tree has been represented metaphorically in an interactive façade. The tree has become a sloping climbing frame made of green oak wood covered with a yellow membrane incorporating plenty of spaces to hide. Kindergarten Somereng and Fjellvegen in Norway by 70°N Arkitektur however was born out of the change of seasons and hours; the architects created settings that grant the children a varied and sensuous experience of the physical surroundings that can fulfill their changing needs. The children can experience their surroundings from height or depth, proximity or distance, and explore a range of spatial differentiations: open, closed, intimate or unlimited. The physical body itself is experienced in motion and stagnation, diagonally, horizontally and vertically. Other designs are more provocative to the eye, such as Fuji Kindergarten by Tezuka Architects in Tokyo which presents a building shape without redundant corners, one that avoids introversion and promotes a sense of community with generous open spaces and clear lines of sight. In the open play areas beneath the flat roof, transitional spaces link the group rooms in a flowing form, and at right angles to these, the building opens out like an umbrella.

//

Kindergartens – Educational Spaces reflects not only the play and innocence of children, but also the designers' inner child.

Tosca, 2 years

Frederik, 7 years

Lara, 5 years

SMALL
150–1000 m²

studio3 - Institute for
Experimental Architecture

↑ | **Outdoor playground**
↗ | **Inclined wall with niches**
→ | **Exterior view**

Olifantsvlei Preschool

34 students built this state-owned preschool building with the help of local workers. The complex consists of two classrooms, kitchen, sanitary installation and an outdoor playground. Embedded in a colorful landscape, adventure and curiosity are encouraged in an experimental space comprising a number of different and undetermined zones. A path meanders across the site via shady spaces, dwelling places and patches of vegetation towards the building in the center and continues through it to the woodland beyond. Inside, the wall design allows for niches, retreats and elevated landings suitable for children. Varying atmospheres and moods are created by well directed lighting through regular openings.

PROJECT FACTS

Address: Lenasia Road, IQ 316 Portions 15 & 27, 1812 Kliptown, Gauteng, Johannesburg, South Africa.
Completion year: 2006. **Gross floor area:** 150 m². **Building capacity:** 80 children.

↑ | **General view**
← | **Classroom**

← | Covered terrace
↙ | Detail wooden wall
↓ | Sections

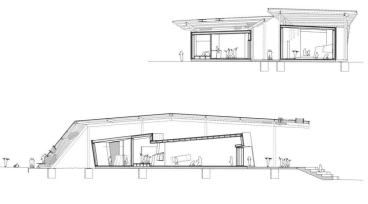

cercadelcielo. studio
architecture

↑ | Main entrance
→ | Wall mounted coat hanger along wall

Kindergarten in Murcia

This kindergarten is dedicated for children of up to three years of age. The façade, as op-posed to the usual building's façade, is composed with the interior of the classrooms; so, the meaning of inhabiting a space is contradicted here by allowing the exterior activities come into the interior. The program is divided into two types of spaces: the "existential areas", classrooms or dining room, learning spaces, play and social areas for the children; and the "soft areas", which are the rest of the functional spaces: lobby, kitchen, storage, sleeping rooms and bathrooms. The interior is composed of three semitransparent boxes, which function as bathrooms and kitchen, with a rather ephemeral material. They are understood as furniture, almost mobile.

Address: Calle Pintor Pedro Flores, Edificio Carmen-Parque, ESC. 7, 30002 Bajo, Murcia, Spain.
Completion year: 2007. **Gross floor area:** 160 m². **Group size:** 24 children.

↑ | Gymnastics room
← | Interior module with acrylic plastic

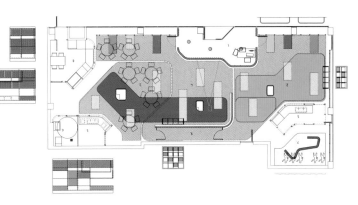

← | Classroom
↑ | Floor plan
↙ | Restroom
↓ | Curved wall surface

AGENCE BECKMANN-N'THÉPÉ ARCHITECTES

↑ | **Activity room**
→ | **Building in landscape**

Les Petits Lardons Nursery

An unusual architecture amid one of Paris's first ZAC development areas, the "Les Petits Lardons" nursery extension scheme is based on a maximalist will, spatial generosity taken to the limit. The final volume is merely the outcome of the available space. A critical, prospective, unqualified architecture with no particular definition, the building imposes itself in its playful modernity, on the scale of the small child. The structural lattices and opacities are handled by a mathematical reading between the interior and the exterior. Inside, a simple contemporary "movable architecture" structures the different sections. It is organized in the most sensitive way between ergonomic and programmatic considerations.

PROJECT FACTS **Address:** 20 rue des Ecluses St Martin, 75010 Paris, France. **Completion year:** 2006. **Gross floor area:** 220 m². **Group size:** 24 children per group.

↑ | View to interior from garden
← | Interior view - reflection

← | Detail of side façade
↙ | Sleeping room
↓ | Elevation

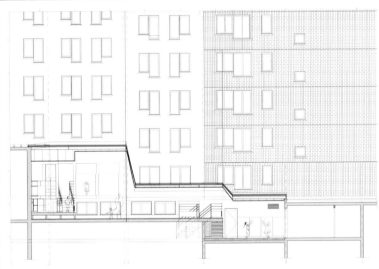

↑ | Classroom
→ | View to green roof

Arreletes Daycare Center

Located on the border between town and countryside and surrounded by a sports area and an orchard, the nursery is composed of two volumes. The lower volume incorporates the classrooms and courtyard and is supported by an existing argricultural wall and the upper volume houses the teachers' offices which overlook the children's courtyard. The interior spaces are versatile, continuous and have controlled lighting. Connected through the changing room to the courtyard, the classrooms enjoy excellent views to the east through the horizontal window that rests on the slope, and a pixelated image of leaves gives the interior corridor screened light from the west.

PROJECT FACTS
Address: Calle Lleida s/n, 25221 Els Alamús, Lleida, Spain. **Completion year:** 2008. **Gross floor area:** 254, 36 m². **Group size:** 16 children.

↑ | **Exterior view by night**
← | **Hallway**

← | Detail façade
↙ | Playground
↓ | Floor plans

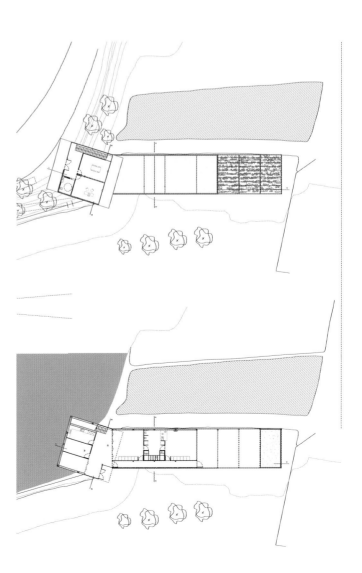

raumhochrosen

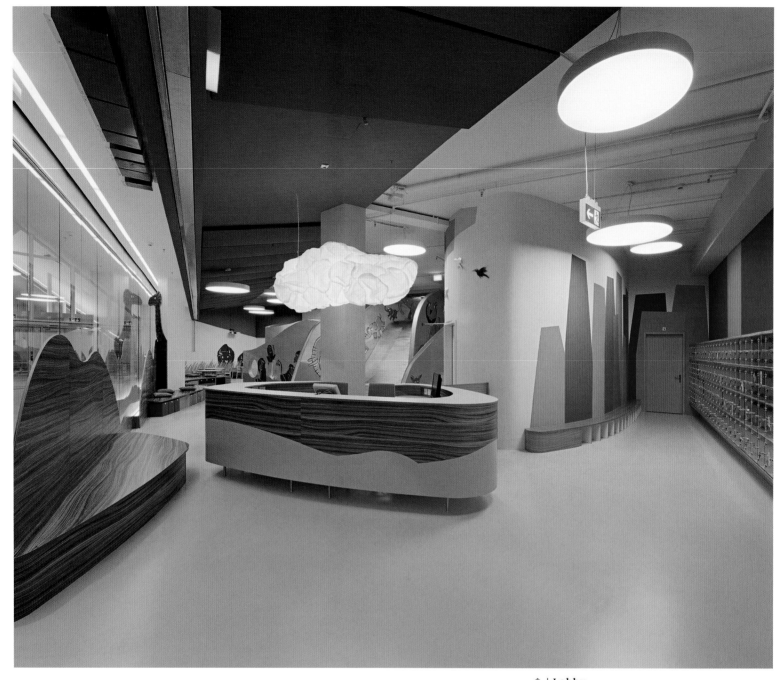

↑ | **Lobby**
→ | **Play area**

Kinderland Westside

The "Kinderland Westside" is located in a shopping center and is designed to occupy about 100 children for up to four hours. This task is accomplished with a varied play landscape extending over two levels. The Kinderland design is inspired by the Savanne. In reference to the many animal illustrations, the two levels depict the animals' habitat. For instance, the entrance to the cloak rooms is conceptualized as a „canyon". In contrast, the green hued reading area creates the impression of a bird's nest in the treetops. In the main section with the crafts area there is a bench with a softly contoured edge of a riverbank, surrounding a sky blue "waterhole".

PROJECT FACTS

Address: Riedbachstrasse 100, 3027 Bern, Switzerland. **Graphic design:** Wohnzimmer – Büro für Gestaltung & Sägenvier. **Completion year:** 2008. **Gross floor area:** 350 m². **Building capacity:** 100 children.

↑ | Reading room
← | Slide in lobby area

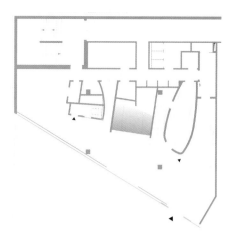

← | Playroom
↑ | Floor plan
↓ | Detail façade by night

↑ | **Wooden terrace**
→ | **Exterior view**

Children in the Garden

Extension Kindergarten Rohrendorf / Krems

In the new construction of the kindergarten, care was taken to encroach as little as possible on the surface of the large-scale garden. The building therefore snuggles tightly into the party wall of the adjoining building. The two group rooms open to the east via large wood sliding doors with skylights opening up to the south. The façade is divided in two: untreated larch on the ground floor and Eternit in the roof landscape area. The wood façade is furnished with „adventure nooks", which the children can use as a playful alternation between inside and outside. The low energy kindergarten uses a water-to-water heat pump for its under floor heating system as well as the existing trees for Southern solar-engergy-regulation.

PROJECT FACTS **Address:** Untere Hauptstrasse 26, 3495 Rohrendorf, Austria. **Completion year:** 2008. **Gross floor area:** 400 m² (two new groups). **Group size:** 25 children.

↑ | Garden
← | Window niche

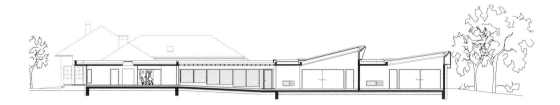

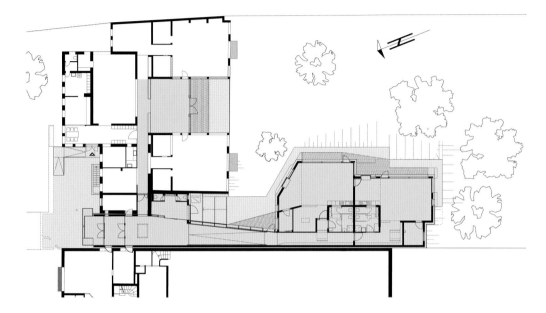

← | Elevation and floor plan
↓ | Hallway

↑ | **Prefabricated massive timber walls and cabinets**
→ | **Interior play area with exposed trusses and vents**

Svartlamoen Nursery

Constructed inside the shell of a derelict car showroom, three wooden "houses" have been built around a central space. These houses are the home bases and work areas for the children. The zones between the "houses" provide the shared facilities, including a biology/ecology room and a large plaza. Outside, a sustainable playing area comprises a large sundeck, orchards, a small farm with sheep and hens, an allotment garden and a mystical forest. All new interior walls are constructed in prefabricated massive timber elements creating an organic wooden "landscape" for the children to explore, a landscape with great contrasts: light and darkness, big and small spaces, solid and transparent surfaces.

↑ | **Kitchen**
← | **Slanted massive timber wall**

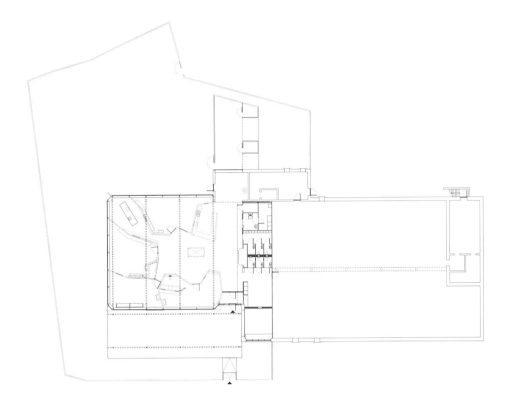

← | Floor plan
↓ | Exterior view

Drost + van Veen
architecten

↑ | Façades partially clad in colored
wooden beams
↗ | Exterior view
→ | Activity room

De Kleine Kikker

The new daycare center is a playful and colorful building overlooking a meadow of grazing sheep and neighboring a traditional farm. Conceived as a contemporary type of farm, the colored façade and aluminium roof contrast the rustic environment, while the silhouette of the pointed roof refers to the existing farm building. Towards the back of the structure, the nursery is transformed into a modernistic, functional building with a flat roof. The organization of the space is simple and logical, yet creates many surprising views from one room into the next. The children's groups are housed in the rear of the building where there is a large balcony creating outdoor space and acting as a sun canopy.

Address: Toulouseaan 43, 3584 Utrecht, Netherlands. **Completion year:** 2003. **Gross floor area:** 520 m². **Number of children's groups:** 4 groups.

↑ | **Front façade**
← | **Staircase with angled ceiling**

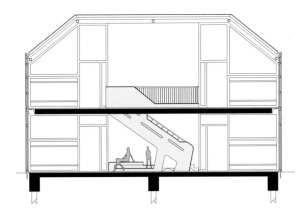

← | Sections
↙ | Group room
↓ | Covered balcony

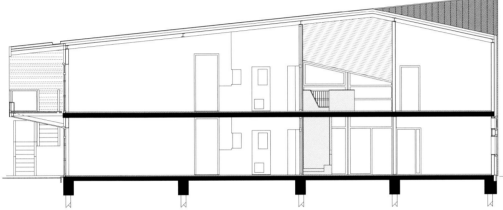

Susanne Hofmann
Architekten. Baupiloten

↑ | Detail large new window
→ | Main external structure - "delving into lemonade"

Taka-Tuka-Land

Pippi Longstocking's "Taka-Tuka-Land" from the book by Astrid Lindgren with the same name served as a model for the building. Pippi's old oak, inside of which lemonade seems to be flowing, is inspired by drawings and models by the children. This "Stream of Lemonade" has seven stations, for instance a panorama window, from which one can already see the "Taka-Tuka-Land" visitors from a distance, as well as a large playroom with many tilted levels to run through. In the spaces, shades of yellow prevail, appearing on the walls as well as on the furnishings. At the last station the stream breaks through the bark, that is the wall of the house, with a play façade in the form of monkey bars for the children.

PROJECT FACTS

Address: Hohenzollernring 93, 13587 Berlin-Spandau, Germany. **Completion year:** 2007. **Gross floor area:** 545 m². **Group size:** 15 children (5 groups).

↑ | **External structure flows into the interior**
← | **Floor plan and axonometry**

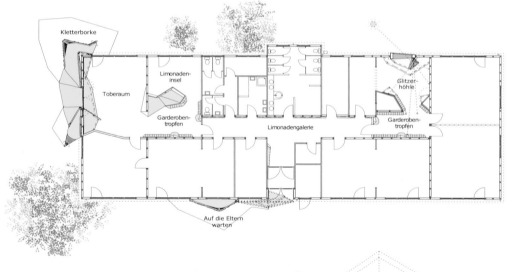

← | Large-scale windows facing garden
↓ | The lemonade continues inside with
seating areas

Pietro Boschetti

↑ | **Exterior side view**
→ | **Seating area in garden**

Nuova Scuola dell'Infanzia Arosio

The design of the kindergarten is oriented to the architectonic figure of the "orto con-cluso", or garden behind walls. The enclosure of the light colored, exposed concrete wall merges in a unity with the two story structure made of the same material. The access to the kindergarten and the function rooms is on the ground floor on the east side and relative to the slope of the grounds lies one floor beneath the garden level. High ribbon windows let daylight into the rooms. The large, light-flooded common rooms are oriented towards the garden, in front of which a terrace, covered by a three meter roof overhang, provides a protected play area for the children.

PROJECT FACTS
Address: 6939 Alto Malcantone, Ticino, Switzerland. **Completion year:** 2006. **Gross floor area:** 560 m². **Group size:** 25 children (2 groups).

↑ | Exterior view from garden
← | Panoramic window

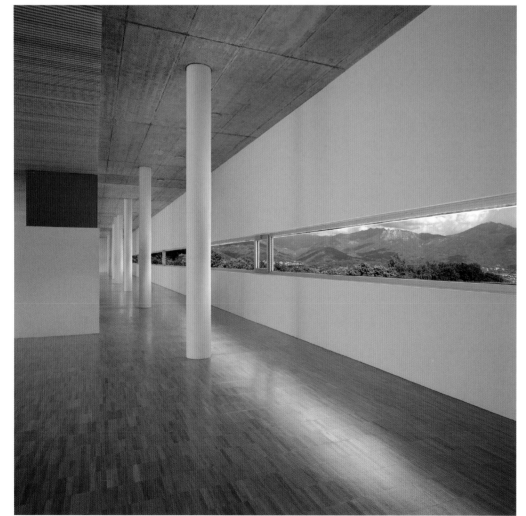

← | Multi-function room
↙↓ | Floor plans

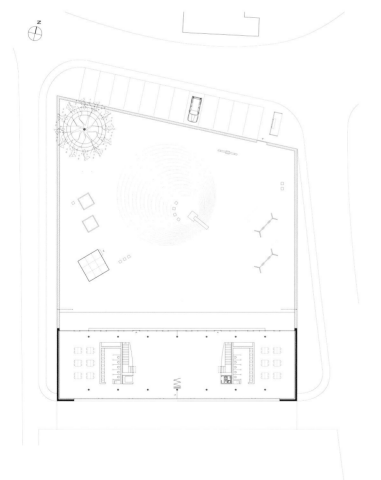

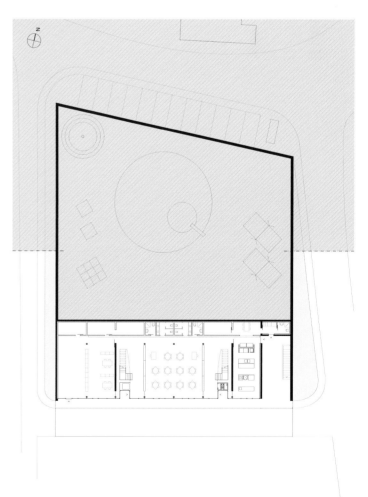

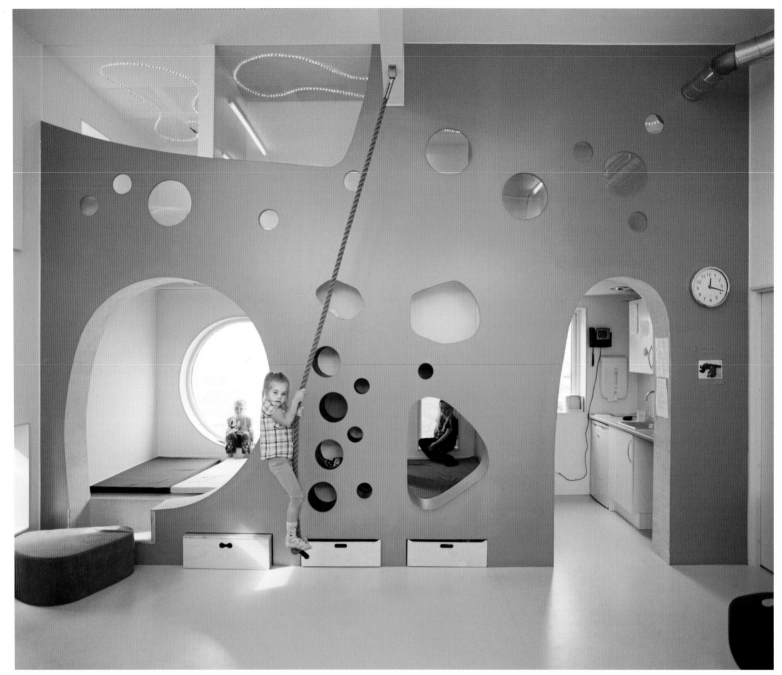

↑ | **Playing wall with climbing wall, peeking/crawling holes**
→ | **Puppet theater section**

Kindergarten Somereng and Fjellvegen

This kindergarten concept is organized in a number of linear zones from a series of roofed outdoor terraces and an "indoor street" with water-play areas and a winter garden feel to intimate reading nooks and mezzanines. These zones enable a soft transition from the exterior to the interior spaces - from the exposed wide landscape to the private and quieter zones. The rooms themselves offer a variety of functions: simple moves can transform the size and feel of each space. Adjustable walls contain a variety of playing elements: pull-out furniture, climbing walls and puppet shows. The concept is an exploration of a child's imaginative world with themes of transition, conversion and surprise.

Location: Tromsø, Norway. **Carpenter and interior:** Duksund Snekkerverksted / G. Schwalenstöcker. **Completion year:** 2006. **Gross floor area:** 622 m².

↑ | Playing and crawling walls
← | Theater/performance area

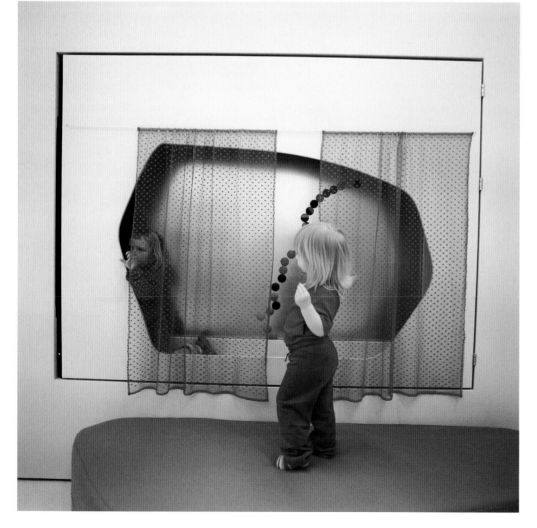

← | Sketch
↓ | Exterior view

Antonio Citterio Patricia Viel
and Partners

↑ | **Night view of the façade overlooking the courtyard**
↗ | **Detail of the South exterior façade**
→ | **Storage room**

Company Nursery

The company nursery in Verona is on the GlaxoSmithKline company campus which is an enclave with a workforce of approximately 1,500 people. The nursery is situated in a highly specialized and technical environment and the project had the object to carve out a domestic space in a semi-urban area made up of industrial buildings and warehouses. The nursery occupies a rectangular site and is arranged around an elongated courtyard with an irregular plan. In this way, the building creates a protected space accommodating the open-air playground. The size of the building enveloping the courtyard varies considerably: the south filiform section is reduced to a portico while the large section to the north houses all the nursery spaces so that the teaching areas and canteen can look onto the courtyard through a large window and also benefit from better lighting.

PROJECT FACTS
57

Address: Via Fleming 2 I, 37135 Verona Italy. **Completion year:** 2005. **Gross floor area:** 690 m².

↑ | Aerial view
← | Group room
↓ | Floor plan

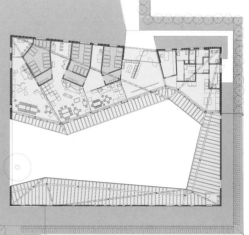

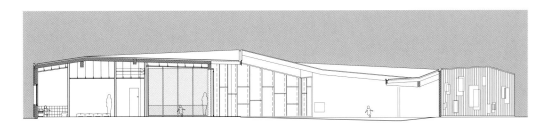

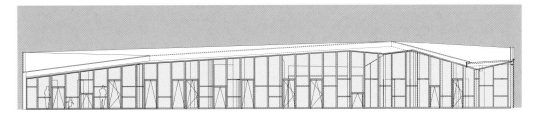

← | Sections and elevations
↓ | South façade

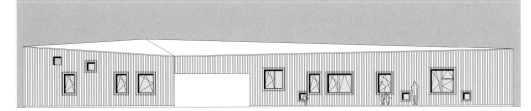

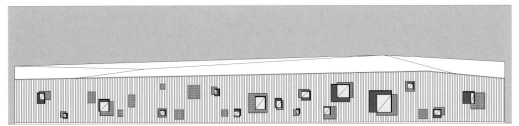

↑ I "Market place" hall
↗ I Exterior view by dusk
→ I Classroom with a storage dividing wall system

Kindergarten Dandelion Clock

The design parameters set by the building owner specified an extremely economical build-ing which could be erected in a short period of time. A series of four repeating building elements were selected for the building's form. These are arranged in the shape of a wind-mill grouped around a central auditorium. The elaborate color concept emphasizes this floor plan. The building is built with timber studding in order to make the most efficient use of the building geometry. The auditorium features a striking skylight, the so-called "Jester's cap". This sets apart the kindergarten from the commercial environs as well as providing a rallying point for the children.

PROJECT FACTS **Address:** Karl-Tschamber-Straße 6, 74722 Buchen im Odenwald, Germany. **Completion year:** 2007. **Gross floor area:** 630 m². **Educational program design for:** Physical or developmental handicaps. **Group size:** 6-8 children (5 groups).

↑ | **North-east exterior view**
← | **Diagrammatic plan sketch**

← | Detail of colorful ceilings
↑ | Conceptual section
↓ | View to landscape from classroom

Elisa Valero Ramos

↑ | **Interior with filtered light**
↗ | **Garden**
→ | **Activity room**

Daycare Center and Municipal Dining Hall Los Mondragones

A vast military block north of Granada has been transformed into an administration complex including a daycare center. The peculiarities of the site, its topography and orientation as well as its specific use, presented a variety of challenges. The daycare center is in three modules and, on the recommendation of a team of pedagogues, is based on the concept of creating spaces that favor learning and the development of psychomotor activity. The classrooms have double lighting and high windows that face the morning sun, while a glass wall to the west opens onto a garden full of plants. Energy consumption was optimized by the installation of thermal insulation and insulation against humidity.

Address: Calle Beiro, Granada, Spain. **Artist:** Joaquin Peña Toro. **Completion year:** 2006. **Gross floor area:** 691 m². **Group size:** 8-20 children (3 groups).

↑ | **Exterior view from street side**
← | **Floor plan**
↙ | **Elevations**

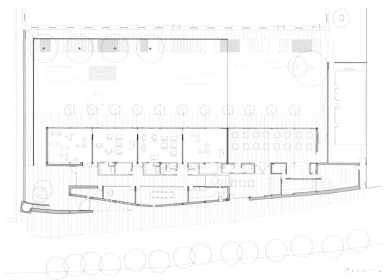

← | Colorful façade
↙ | Indoor garden
↓ | Hallway with sliding wall elements

Bernardo Bader

↑ | Classroom with open floor plan
↗ | Classroom with view to landscape
→ | Hallway

Kindergarten Bizau

The situation at hand in Bizau is marked by impressive views into the mountainous region of the Bregenz forest. The newly built kindergarten creates a natural integration into the built environment and an avenue to the mountainous region. It is conceived as a timber structure, with a façade consisting of a facing of silver fir. The generously proportioned windows permit a view into the spacious interior structure, built entirely of local fir and ash. The quality of the wood is augmented by criteria like pollutant free indoor air and an exceptional life cycle assessment. The building thereby makes a contribution to the subject of regionality, environmental compatibility and ecology.

PROJECT FACTS   **Address:** Kirchdorf 371, 6874 Bizau, Austria. **Completion year:** 2009. **Gross floor area:** 720 m². **Group size:** 20 children (2 groups).

↑ | Classroom with view to surroundings
← | Site plan

← | Activities room
↓ | Exterior view

Taku Sakaushi + Chika Kijima / O.F.D.A.

↑ | Playground
→ | Corridor connecting old and new buildings

Suruga Kindergarten

The project involved renovating and partially rebuilding an existing kindergarten which was composed of three buildings, one of which had to be entirely replaced. Eight classrooms are located on the first and second floors ķind the third floor houses a meeting room and balcony with a small pool. It was necessary to install a corridor connecting the buildings, but this would prevent sunlight and ventilation from entering the classrooms. The solution was to make the corridor a translucent façade with additional windows. Over the steel frame, polycarbonate panels with a honeycomb profile were installed and fitted in random positions and shapes to create a more vibrant and fun environment.

PROJECT FACTS **Address:** Fuji, Shizuoka Prefecture, Japan. **Completion year:** 2005. **Gross floor area:** 1139 m². **Group size:** 28 children (13 groups).

↑ | Classrooms on second floor
← | Multipurpose room

← | Corridor covered with a translucent façade
↓ | Interior classroom

Stifter + Bachmann

↑ | Interior second floor
→ | Southern façade by night

Kindergarten Niederdorf, Reconstruction & Extension

The existing kindergarten in a Wilhelminian era villa dating from 1906 was renovated and augmented with a linear, two-story annex. At floor height the new structure is oriented to the old building and the two are connected by a narrow glass caesura. The street side of the building is more closed, but opens up expansively on the south side to the sun, the river and its luxurious bank vegetation. The façade is a simple composition of triple glazings and wood panels alternatingly installed between the floor slabs. The whole kindergarten is usable without obstruction and in addition has the use of an in-house kitchen, a multi-purpose and exercise room and a Kneipp facility.

PROJECT FACTS

Address: Rienzstrasse 16, 39030 Niederdorf, South Tyrol, Italy. **Completion year:** 2008. **Gross floor area:** 800 m². **Educational approach:** Holistic learning theory. **Group size:** 20-25 children (3 groups).

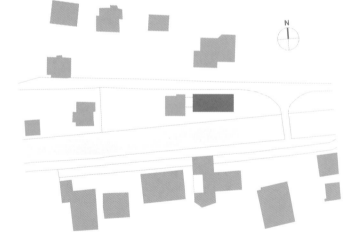

↑ | **View from river**
← | **Site plan**
↙ | **Floor plan**

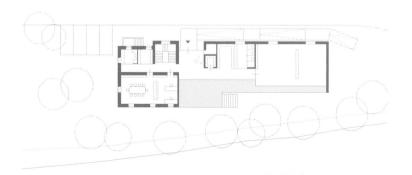

← | Washroom
↓ | Group room

↑ | **View from hallway to classroom and across to garden**
→ | **Entrance with skylights**

Kindergarten Deutsch-Wagram

The one story structure is situated on the northern boundary of the property, in order to open it to the south and expose the garden to the sun for the whole day. All rooms are accessed via a large hall, directly lit by a skylight and indirectly by a porch, open cloakrooms and covered terraces. The large area glazing of the group rooms in the south provides a considerable passive solar benefit and copious daylight. An awning with photovoltaic elements and exterior blinds provides shade in summer. The building is heated by a groundwater heat pump, with additional heat from thermal collectors gathered in a buffer storage.

PROJECT FACTS Address: Robert Blum-Straße 47a, 2232 Deutsch-Wagram, Austria. **Completion year:** 2009. **Gross floor area:** 818 m². **Number of groups:** 4 groups.

↑ | Backyard
← | Classroom

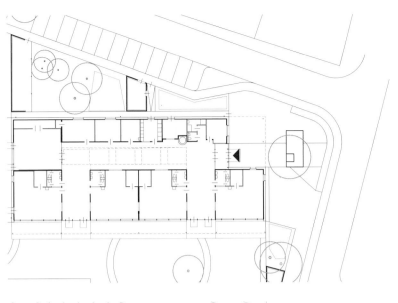

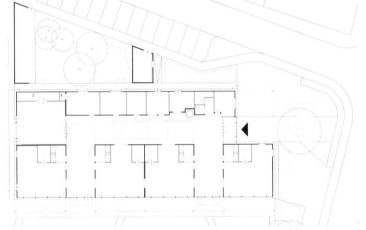

← | Floor plans
↓ | Main entrance

Marcio Kogan

↑ | Backyard with old wooden house
→ | Exterior view by night

Berçário Primetime

The project aims to incorporate the specifics of a nursery program while seeking creative space solutions. Circulation is achieved using ramps and child-friendly materials such as soft flooring, and focuses on operational ergonometry to create a safe and comfortable environment. The technical team followed the same orientation, offering optimal solutions for the best air and water quality, floor heating and balanced lighting. The landscaping was equally conceived to guarantee safe interaction among children. In addition to using natural materials, the colors yellow, orange and red were selected to create a stimulating atmosphere.

PROJECT FACTS
Address: São Paulo, Brazil. **Interior design:** Diana Radomysler + Regiane Leão. **Completion year:** 2007.
Gross floor area: 870 m². **Building capacity:** 75 children (2 groups).

↑ | **Detail of stacked volumes**
← | **Interior playroom**
↓ | **Floor plans**

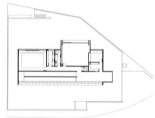

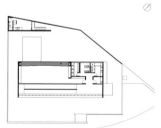

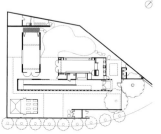

← | Detail of alveolar poly-carbonate window-frame
↓ | Exterior view by night

Béal & Blanckaert
architectes associés

↑ | Front façade   ↓ | Section
↓ | Floor plan

Maison de la Petite Enfance
St Saulve

The suburban nursery of St Sualve comprises a gathering of pavilions and towers and is characterized by the presence of many trees. A series of connected pavilions are covered with thin, sloping, stainless steel roofs that generate a variety of interior spaces to be used for a variety of functions. The plan is organized around two buildings, whose opaque and open frontages are engaged in dialogue with one other. This dialectic functions as a symbolic representation of the fruitful and open discussion regarding this project between the client and the architect, each of whom contributed their own recommendations and thoughts.

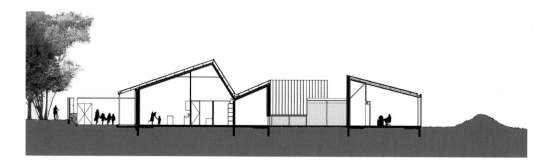

PROJECT FACTS **Address:** Avenue Schumann St Saulve, France. **Completion year:** 2002. **Gross floor area:** 870 m². **Group size:** 15 children (2 groups).

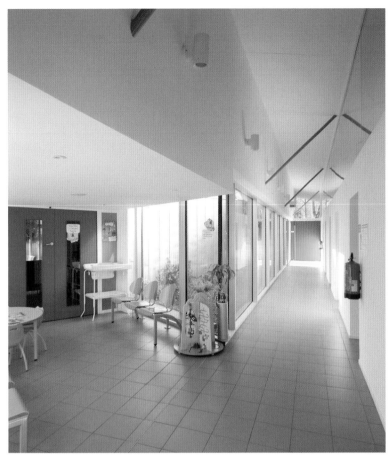

↑ | Hallway with sloping ceiling

↑ | Pavilion covered with sloping roof
↓ | View to building wings from courtyard

↑ | **View from garden to iluminated interior**
→ | **Stonewall linking building structures**

Nursery School in Covolo di Pederobba

Hidden among the vineyards and wheatfields, the Nursery School in Covolo comprises a collection of modest structures linked by a continuous series of stone walls. The new building forms an enclosure that both embraces and allows itself to be defined by the features of the landscape. A rough concrete wall is colored to match the surrounding landscape, reflecting light in various ways. The wall opens to the south, revealing the massive structure, before retracting and doubling, coloring itself to emphasize its passages. The overhang, the stabilized gravel paving and the lighting transform the threshold into a space where classroom spaces and garden meet and form the imagination of a possible world.

PROJECT FACTS   91

Address: Covolo di Pederobba, Treviso, Italy. **Completion year:** 2006. **Gross floor area:** 900 m².

↑ | Interior courtyard
← | Main entrance

← | Large window in multi-function room
↓ | Glass façade connecting interior and exterior

RCR Aranda Pigem Vilalta
arquitectes

↑ | Courtyard
→ | View to semi-transparent colored glass

Els Colors Kindergarten

Formed from the juxtaposition and overlap of a series of simple pieces that differ only
in color, this kindergarten is designed from the perspective of a child who is developing
skills of orientation and spatial awareness. Interior spaces flow into one another with few
boundaries enabling the children to learn about spatial relationships. Two rectangular,
single level sections connected by a covered passageway house the classrooms, communal areas and cafeteria, while a taller section located above the main entrance is used as
multi-functional space. Concrete is used for the horizontal elements, steel for the vertical
structural elements and colored glass for the semi-transparent walls.

PROJECT FACTS
Address: Carrer del Ter, 54, 08560 Manlleu (Barcelona), Spain. **Completion year:** 2004. **Gross floor area:** 928 m². **Group size:** 15 children.

↑ | Multi-function room
← | Sections

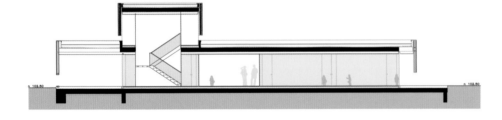

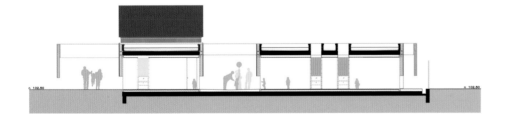

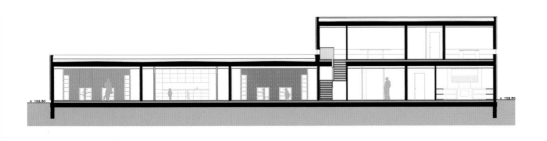

← | Meeting room
↓ | Children's restrooms

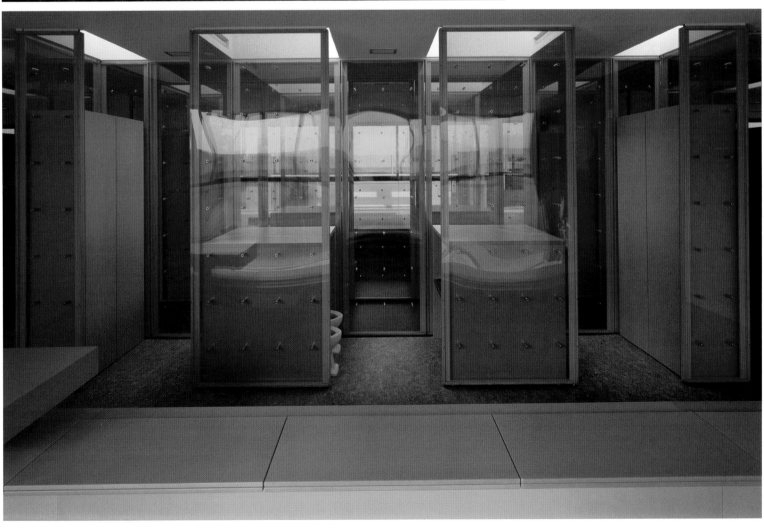

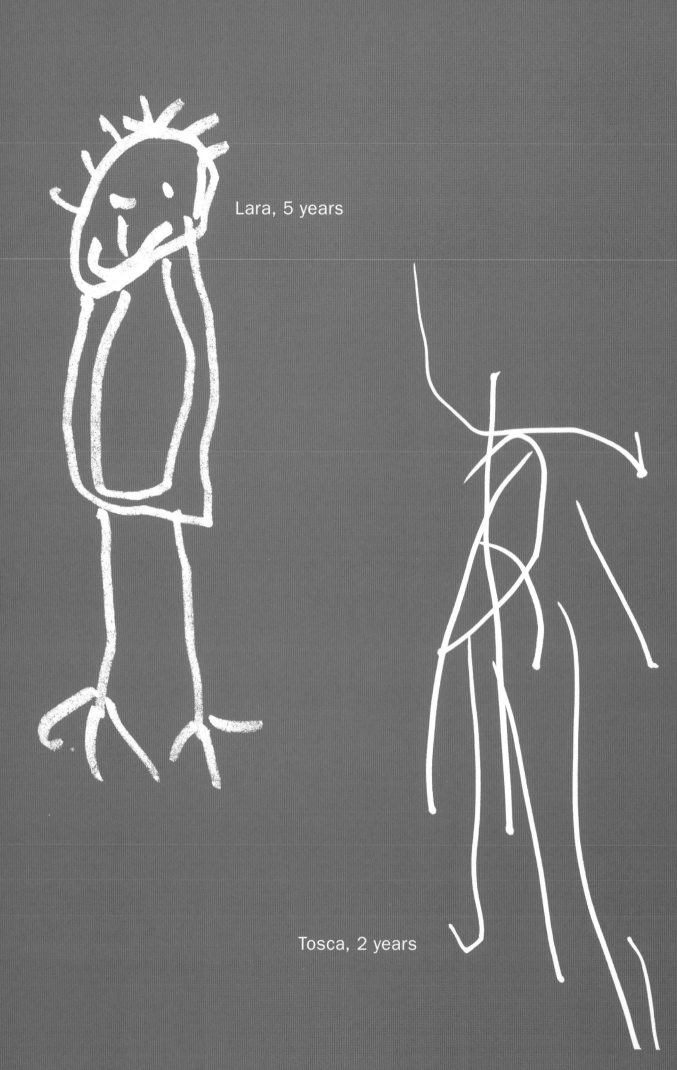

Lara, 5 years

Tosca, 2 years

Frederik, 7 years

MEDIUM
1000–1500 m²

↑ | **Multi-function exercise room**
→ | **Detail of oversized "grass blades"**
façade

Kindergarten Sighartstein

The two story rectangular kindergarten is located in the middle of green meadows and fields. The first on site impression suggests the concept of the constructed playground. The raised, abstractly stylized "grass" façade of the cubic buildings encompasses the volumes, at the same time lending identity and orientation to the kindergarten. Two kindergarten groups are housed on the ground floor, while the two toddler groups are located on the upper floor. All group rooms face the sunny southern side, with the ancillary areas on the north side. The centerpiece of the buildings, the multi-function exercise room, connects the kindergarten with the toddler group.

PROJECT FACTS
Address: Sighartstein 37, 5202 Neumarkt am Wallersee, Austria. **Completion year:** 2009. **Gross floor area:** 1,000 m². **Group size:** 25 children (4 groups).

↑ | **Activity room with double-height ceiling**
← | **Sections and elevations**

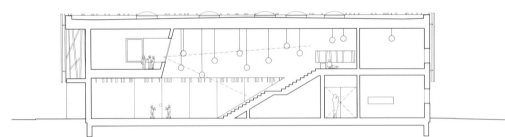

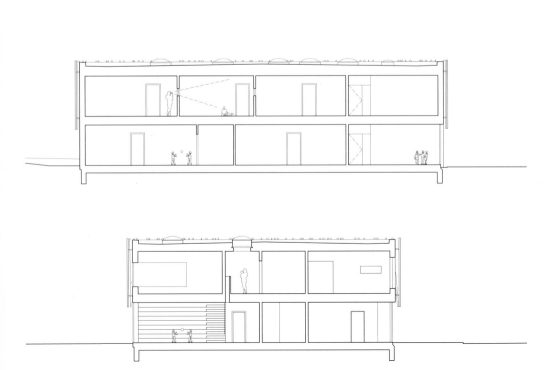

← | Detail façade
↓ | Garden with outdoor eating area

Lev-Gargir Architects

↑ | View to indoor play area from terrace
→ | Gymnastics area

Kindergarten in Ramat Hasharon

Situated in a satellite suburb of Tel Aviv, this kindergarten was created from the desire to apply to children's physical surroundings the educational principles that are at the foundation of its activities - respect and equality among children and the opportunity to play and explore new acticvities in intimate spaces. The design was inspired by Bauhaus concepts: simple and clean forms, long and open views throughout the project and horizontal and minimalist lines. This simplicity allows the children complete imaginative freedom in their environment. Finishing materials such as white plaster, exposed white masonry bricks and large windows complete the serenity of the design.

PROJECT FACTS

Address: Ramat Hasharon, Tel Aviv, Israel. **Interior & furniture design:** Sarit Shani Hay. **Completion year:** 2009. **Gross floor area:** 1,000 m².

↑ | Drawing room
← | Playing and crawling walls
↓ | Floor plan

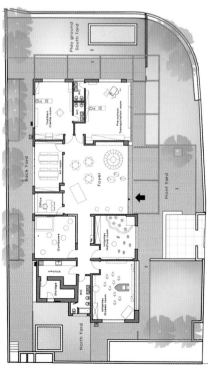

← | Interior view to wooden car
↓ | Interior play area

D'Inka Scheible Hoffmann
Architekten BDA

↑ | **Inner-covered courtyard**
→ | **Outdoor space**

Crèche Schwieberdingen

The former Posthof building with its sprawling paved depot surfaces was converted into a kindergarten. The new appearance is marked by one story annexes and a new façade design. An ensemble with various spatial arrangements has emerged from a single building. The recreation and group rooms open to the south, each with its own open area on the terrace. The especially generous play area on the east side extends to the floodplain of the Glems. Ample daylight and transparent transitions lend a children friendly atmosphere to the building. The wood building material also contributes to the look of the building.

PROJECT FACTS

Address: Herrenwiesenweg 9, 71701 Schwieberdingen, Germany. **Completion year:** 2008. **Gross floor area:** 1,038 m². **Educational approach:** Open concept after Emmi Pikler and INFANS concept. **Group size:** 10 children (6 groups).

↑ | **Exterior view**
← | **Hallway**

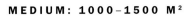

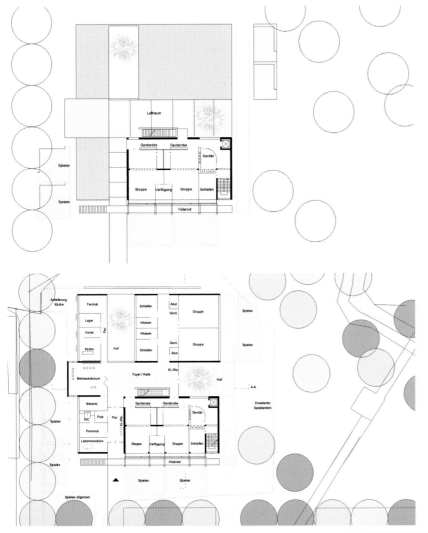

← | Floor plans
↓ | Group room

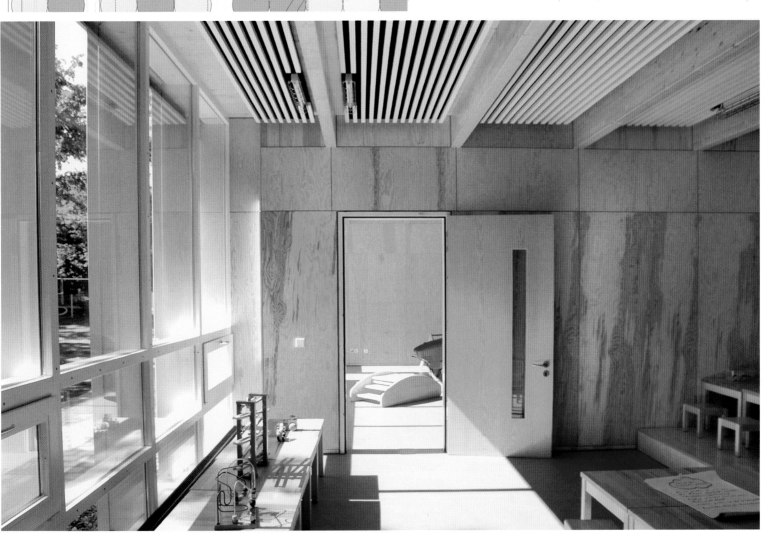

Marc Eller Architekten

↑ | Playground
→ | Stairs with slide

Enterprise Crèche of the Metro Group

The broad arching roof is supported by thin steel pillars. It spans the building sections and protects the reddish brown larch façade from the weather. A light glass membrane surrounds the one story "Kitchen House", making a part of this roofed-over area into a closed play area for the children. The stairway to the upper floor was partially formed as sitting steps. In the middle is a slide, which is enclosed on both sides by an odiously green snake which winds its way to the upper story, where it sticks out its red tongue, which can be used as a seat. There are two openings in the belly of the snake, through which children can gain access to the slide.

PROJECT FACTS

Address: Altenbergstraße 97, 40235 Düsseldorf, Germany. **Completion year:** 2007. **Gross floor area:** 1,044 m². **Group size:** 16 children (4 groups).

↑ | **View to main entrance**
← | **Floor plans**

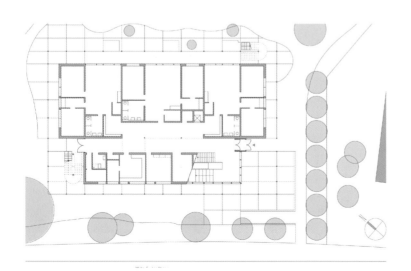

← | Activity room
↓ | Crawling snake on second floor

Dorte Mandrup Arkitekter

↑ | Front façade by night
→ | Rooftop play area

Daycare Center
Skanderborggade

Located in a neighborhood of dense urban blocks, this new three unit daycare institution/ nursery school was restricted to one story by the district zoning plan. It was therefore necessary to place the required outdoor areas largely on the roof. The building consists of two planes which extend to the boundaries of the site. The ground terrain surface is folded upwards to form a slope between the ground and the roof. The slope angle offers the best sun exposure to both the slope and the courtyard from the south and the west. A forest of columns to be used for swings and other forms of play is located underneath the slope. Two light wells cut into the roof plane allow the interior to be naturally lit.

PROJECT FACTS
Address: Krausesgade 17, 2100 Copenhagen, Denmark. **Completion year:** 2005. **Gross floor area:** 1,045 m². **Group size:** 12 children (3 groups).

↑ | **View to building slope**
← | **Floor plan and sections**

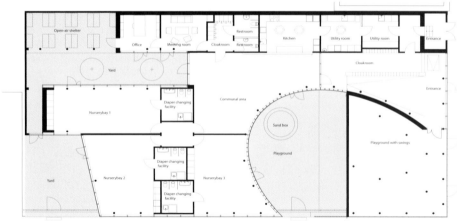

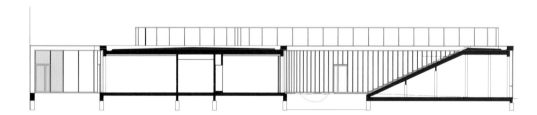

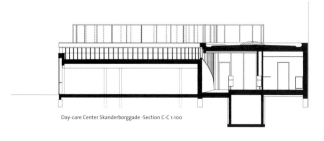

Day-care Center Skanderborggade -Section C-C 1:100

← | Detail rooftop
↓ | Rooftop play area

MPH architectes

↑ | **Entrance area**
↓ | **Floor plan and Section**

Espace de vie enfantine
de Carfagni-Chateaubriand

The building located on the periphery of the park has a pavilion like form. The kindergarten is organized like a little village, whose individual houses are connected with each other by a central space. The group rooms open up to the park by means of large-scale glass panels like loggias. Large terraced seating leads to the roof, which is furnished with open spaces and opportunities to play. The quiet rooms and sanitary facilities are located in the small, reddish orange glazed wood panelled houses. At the same time they constitute the load bearing elements. The parquet flooring creates unity between the common areas and the individual group rooms. Colorful linoleum provides a variegated color scheme in the houses.

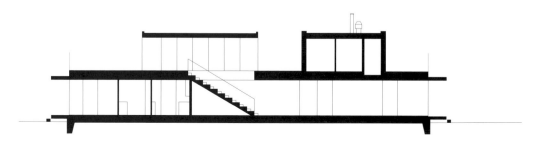

PROJECT FACTS Address: Place Châteaubriand 2, 1202 Geneva, Switzerland. **Completion year:** 2005. **Gross floor area:** 1,060 m². **Group size:** 12-16 children per group (5 groups).

↑ | Interior

↑ | Exterior play area
↓ | Interior with dividing shelf

↑ | Main hall
→ | Rear façade

Ajurinmäki Daycare Center

This daycare center comprises three separate "home areas" for different groups, as well as an open-door daycare center. Construction was confined to the southward sloping side of the plot where the climatic and construction conditions were most favourable. The building has the shape of an organic, living entity feeding the imagination, in the shadow of which the yard opens up towards the south. The interiors vary in height and utilize the attic space below the shallow roof planes. Children are offered a range of opportunities to both explore and observe the surrounding natural environment, while the buidling itself operates as a nature kaleidoscope with a diversity of materials and colors.

PROJECT FACTS
Address: Porarinkatu 9, 2650 Espoo, Finland. **Landscape architect:** Soile Heikkinen. **Completion year:** 2009. **Gross floor area:** 1,065 m². **Group size:** 22 children (3 groups).

↑ | **Backyard**
← | **Entrance hallway**

← | Interior classroom
↓ | Floor plan

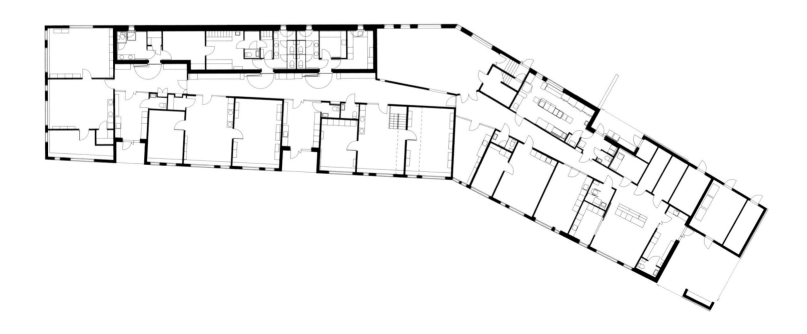

Aeby & Perneger

↑ | Exterior view
↗ | Playroom
→ | Classroom

Crèche de Bernex

The one story building reminds one of a garden pavilion. Most of the rooms are located on the ground floor, some others are in the basement, which is partially exposed to natural light by narrow ribbon windows. In contrast to the clear lines of the exterior design, free form prevails in the interior. Muted daylight is led into the kindergarten in the heart of the building by means of an ellipsoid, translucent body. Erected on a concrete foundation, the wooden structure of the kindergarten is wrapped in a finely lined glass façade. Large sliding windows at full ceiling height open up the structure to the surrounding nature. The building conforms to the Swiss Minergie standard.

PROJECT FACTS

Address: Chemin du Signal 5, 1233 Bernex, Switzerland. **Completion year:** 2007. **Gross floor area:** 1,065 m². **Group size:** 10-15 children (8 groups).

↑ | **Terrace**
← | **Playroom with view to terrace**

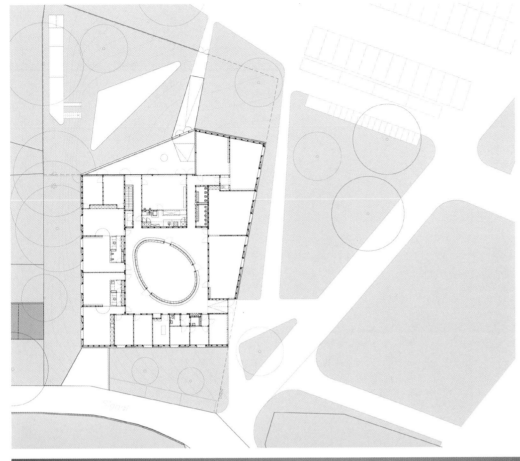

← | Floor plan
↓ | Giant column with shoe storage area

Schneider & Lengauer
Architekten

↑ | Detail of wrap-around window
→ | View into classroom

Kindergarten Neumarkt

The new structure next to the existing kindergarten from the 1990s is architectonically independent from the older structure in terms of form and color. In summer the green façade made of Welleternit harmonizes with the gardens and meadows in the environs and in winter provides a splash of color in the snowscape. On the south side the building leans out over the steeply sloped property, exposing the interior rooms to as much sun as possible. The broad window band, which is adjusted to the height of a child, looks out expansively on the hilly landscape. The white oiled spruce ceiling creates a light atmosphere which the children find cheerful.

PROJECT FACTS
Address: Schulstraße 16, 4212 Neumarkt im Mühlkreis, Austria. **Completion year:** 2006. **Gross floor area:** 1,065 m². **Group size:** 90 children (4 groups).

↑ | Detail glass façade
← | Classroom

← | Stairs to mezzanine level
↙ | Classroom
↓ | Corridor with coat hangers

Béal & Blanckaert
architectes associés

↑ | **Main entrance**
→ | **Enclosed garden**

Maison de la Petite Enfance
St Quentin

Béal & Blanckaert's St Quentin kindergarten is situated near the city center in a dense urban neighborhood. Its brick outer walls form a continuation of the existing street walls, allowing the kindergarten to blend into its surroundings and retain privacy. Within, however, a large rectangular courtyard and garden offer relief from those surroundings through the use of glass and wood, which generate an atmosphere of transparency, modernity and opportunity. A variety of volumes housing a nursery, toy library and logistics center are generated by the contemporary composition of the structure. The units are connected via the outdoor area, accessed through large glass doors.

PROJECT FACTS

Address: Boulevard Victor Hugo St Quentin. **Artist:** Laurent Zimny. **Completion year:** 2002. **Gross floor area:** 1,092 m². **Group size:** 12 children (3 groups).

↑ | **Courtyard**
← | **Floor plan**

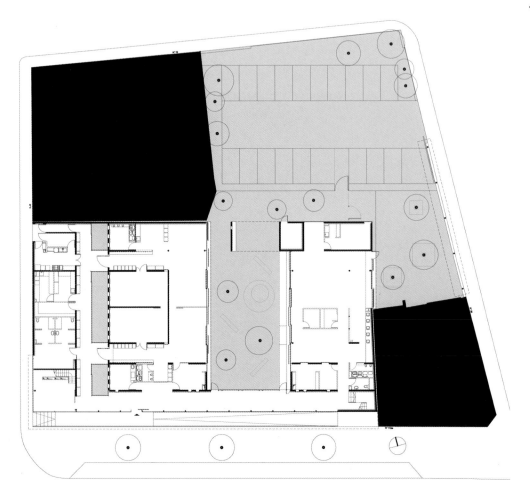

← | Building passage
↓ | Exterior view

Takaharu+Yui Tezuka
Architects

↑ | Aerial view
↗ | Roof as play area
→ | View to playground from interior

Fuji Kindergarten

Built to replace an existing kindergarten, the oval shape arose out of a desire to create a space without dead ends and without segregated or hidden spaces. All spaces are in full view of each other and rooms are divided only by stacked-up furniture, like building blocks. Soft paulownia wood is the primary building material and prevents injury to the children. Rather than installing play equipment, it was decided that the roof itself, with comfortable seating on the eaves, sloping surfaces and skylights, would itself be the play equipment, encouraging children to play creatively. The kindergarten is entirely open for most of the year, creating a fluidity between exterior and interior spaces.

Address: 2-7-1 Kamisuna-cho, Tachikawa, Tokyo, Japan. **Completion year:** 2007. **Gross floor area:** 1,095 m².

↑ | Oval shaped roof as playground
← | Slide connecting roof with playground

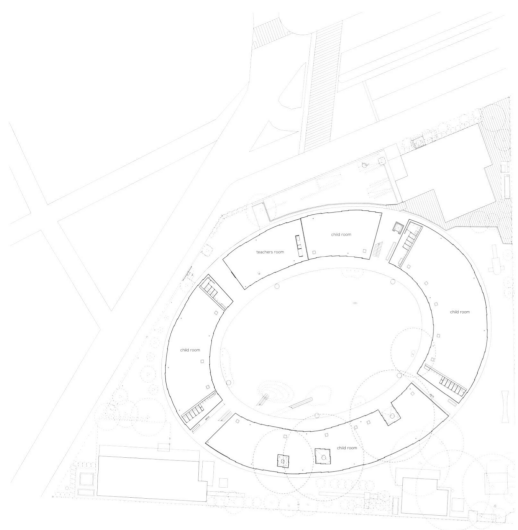

← | Floor plan
↓ | View from covered terrace to play-
ground

C. F. Møller Architects

↑ | Exterior view, with play-ramp access to upper level
→ | Interior of main space, with play-ramps and stage

Children's House Dragen

The integrated kindergarten "Dragen" sets new standards as a sustainable and pedagogically conceived design using largely "Nordic Swan" eco-labelled components. The simple and clear architecture has two levels, linked by staircases and ramps designed to stimulate and challenge the children's sensory and motor skills. Dragen has small niches distributed throughout, to play, read or just withdraw. In addition, there are purpose-built spaces, giving the children special opportunities: a small theater, atelier, motor skills room and pedagogical kitchens indoors and out. Another feature are small "loopholes" in the walls, allowing the children to play across the room divisions.

PROJECT FACTS

Address: Dragebakken, Sanderum, 5000 Odense, Denmark. **Artist:** Lene Barnkob Kaas. **Completion year:** 2009. **Gross floor area:** 1,100 m². **Group size:** 22 kindergarten and 11 nursery children (2 kindergarten and 4 nursery groups).

↑ | Wall with multiple windows at children's heights
↙ | 3D section

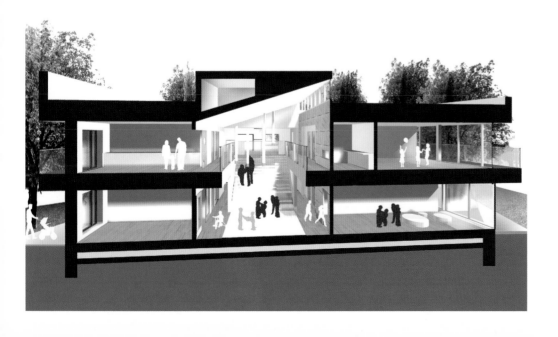

← | Dining room
↓ | Playground with sandbox

Dietrich Untertrifaller
Architekten

↑ | South-oriented glass façade
→ | Wooden platform opens into play garden

Kindergarten Egg

The building augments two existing school facilities. It frames the west side of the square, shielding the adjacent parking area with a wall and opening up to the garden in the south. In order that the rooms do not become overheated because of the large scale glass fronts, a robust structural framework shades them, serving at the same time as a gantry spanning the access path. The upper story, a little less than half the size of the ground floor, juts out to the east, shielding its own access as well as that of the kindergarten. The group rooms are on the ground floor while the large music room, lit by ribbon windows facing north, is located on the upper floor.

PROJECT FACTS

Address: Pfister 825, 6863 Egg, Austria. **Completion year:** 2004. **Gross floor area:** 1,130 m². **Group size:** 15 children (2 groups).

↑ | Exterior view
← | Exposed concrete wall and wooden
façade

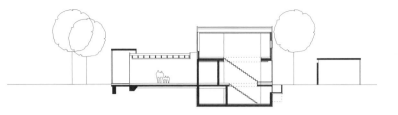

← | Access path
↑ | Section
↓ | Dining room

Hamonic + Masson

↑ | **Exterior view from street side**
→ | **Entrance way**

Crèche and Early Childhood Center

Located at the heart of a working-class quarter in the midst of redevelopment, Hamonic et Masson's crèche represents the municipality's desire for urban transformation. Several services dedicated to early childhood are grouped together, providing an environment for the children's first social interactions and the first steps on the path of education. This is represented in the building's form: a ribbon, open at both ends, beckoning the public to enter while cradling the classrooms within. The classrooms give onto courtyards and play areas, providing a sequence of colorful but introverted spaces, while the generous entry and triumphant first floor window lend a very public nature to the building.

PROJECT FACTS **Address:** Avenue de Grammont 16, 76100 Rouen, France. **Completion year:** 2007. **Gross floor area:** 1,144 m².

↑ | **Front façade**
← | **Floor plans**

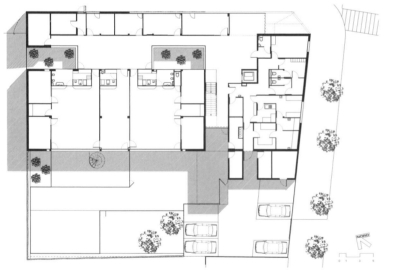

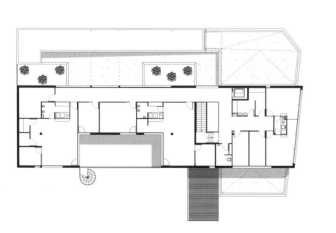

← | Stairs leading to play areas
↓ | Entrance way with inner garden

ccdstudio (Ciutti Ciaffoni
Di Marcantonio)

↑ | Interior classroom
↗ | Exterior view from garden
→ | Terrace

Kindergarten Barbapapà

Located on a hill on the city outskirts, this kindergarten accommodates 60 children in
four classrooms. The project responds to the natural environment of the Emilia Romagna
region by expressing through its architecture a consciousness of the importance of sus-
tainability, which is then transmitted to the children. A green deck ensures excellent thermal insulation, while integrated green areas reduce the visual impact of the volume. Glass
openings are strategically placed along the façade to control the infiltration of light and
heat from the sun at different times of the day. The colors, materials and forms all express
a sustainable system in a consistent contemporary architectural language.

PROJECT FACTS **Address:** via Don Pellegrini, Vignola (Modena), Italy. **Completion year:** 2009. **Gross floor area:** 1,158 m². **Educational approach:** Project-based. **Building capacity:** 60 children.

↑ | Building incorporated into the site
↙ | Diagrams

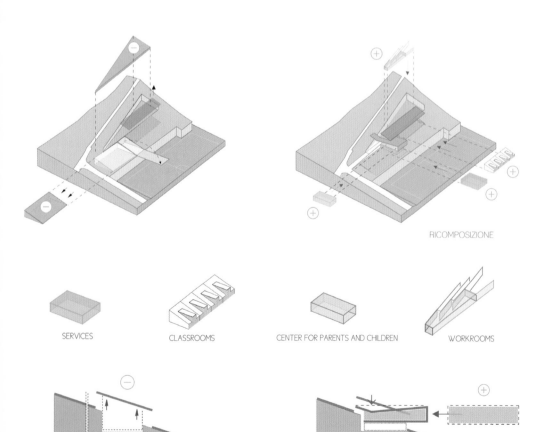

RICOMPOSIZIONE

SERVICES   CLASSROOMS   CENTER FOR PARENTS AND CHILDREN   WORKROOMS

← | Playroom with extended views towards garden
↓ | View to sleeping and playroom

↑ | Backyard
↓ | View to main entrance

↓ | Corridor with lightwell

Children's Day Home Schukowitzgasse

The kindergarten is an urban developmental extension of an existing school. An atrium has been created by displacing the positions of the two building components. The group rooms, which open up to the sun and the garden, are presented to the south of a central hall topped by a large skylight. The function rooms are located in the northern structure. The building materials as well as the entire building services, like the plumbing, are exposed and visible to the building users. The kindergarten is heated by means of a ventilation system. This passive house concept is augmented by the heavy mass of the building, with intensive exploitation of passive solar heating and a large solar hot water system.

Address: Schukowitzgasse 87, Vienna, Austria. **Completion year:** 2006. **Gross floor area:** 1,180 m². **Number of groups:** 6 groups.

↑ | **Multi-function room with view to garden**

↑ | **Side view**
↓ | **Classroom**

Johannes Wiesflecker

↑ | Aerial view
↗ | Front façade
→ | Exterior with view towards overhanging upper floor

Pupil's Crèche Kaysergarten

The building extending along the existing wall is interposed between the heavily traveled street and the fantastic landscape. The overhanging upper floor and its organically shaped terrace on the interior emphasize the transition to nature. In the upper floor the three teaching and group spaces are oriented in three different cardinal directions in direct reference to the exterior space. The floor extends along a parabola shaped terrace around an existing small copse of trees. On the ground floor the spaces are laid out for general use. The glass surfaces of the façade also open the building to the garden, where the children can take advantage of an additional roofed-over play area.

PROJECT FACTS

Address: Innstraße 113a, 6020 Innsbruck, Austria. **Completion year:** 2008. **Gross floor area:** 1,195 m². **Group size:** 30 children (3 groups).

↑ | Foyer
← | Recreational room

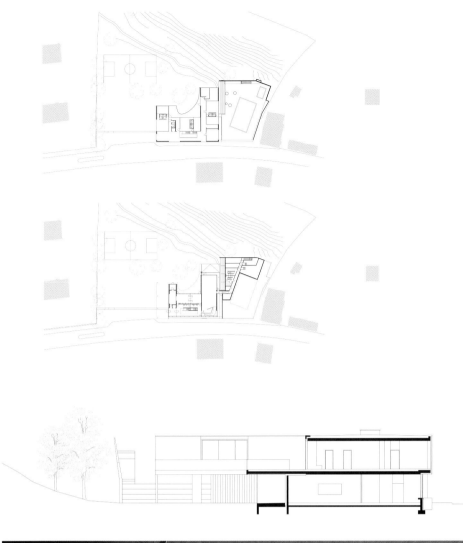

← | Floor plans and elevation
↓ | Group room

Bonnard Woeffray
Architectes

↑ | **Exterior view from rear garden**
→ | **Detail of colorful façade**

La Tonkinelle

The day nursery in Monthey is located in the Parc de Cinquantoux. Its organic form fuses with the park, offering interior spaces with flexible usage. The structure houses six different group spaces on two floors. Each space has an individual character, depending on its location in the building. Variously positioned windows in identical format facilitate different perceptions of the surroundings. The surface design is inspired by the color world of children. Lamellae on the wood façade are graduated in bright luminescent shades of pink, orange, red and green. The shades of color in the ceilings and floors lend a rhythm to the interior space, which simultaneously defines the various group spaces.

PROJECT FACTS

Address: Avenue de la Gare 58, Parc Cinquantoux, 1870 Monthey, Switzerland. **Completion year:** 2008. **Gross floor area:** 1,200 m². **Educational approach:** Emmi Pikler concept. **Group size:** 10–18 children (6 groups).

↑ | Children's play road
← | Pink group space

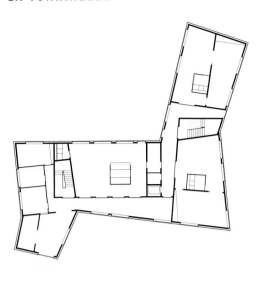

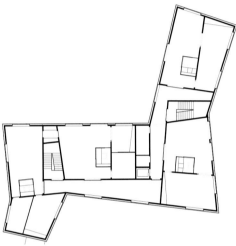

← | Floor plans
↓ | Orange group space

Hans Finner Architekt +
Carroquino Arquitectos

↑ | **Interior view**
→ | **Bird's eye view**

Oliver Kindergarten

Underneath the planted roof landscape play and adventure spaces of various sizes emerge. These are specifically adapted to the needs of children from the ages of three months to three years and offer generous spaces for larger events, as well as areas of retreat for the littlest ones. They are connected by the broad play hallway flanked by function rooms. With only a few openings in the massive outer wall which surrounds the building the structure looks introverted. All play rooms and halls open up at full room height to the three incisioned parallel positioned inner courtyards, ensuring intimacy but still allowing for the opportunity to communicate with the exterior space.

PROJECT FACTS
Address: Calle Antonio Leyva s/n, Zaragoza, Spain. **Completion year:** 2007. **Gross floor area:** 1,200 m². **Group size:** 15 children (6 groups).

↑ | Courtyard
← | Interior group room
↓ | Floor plan

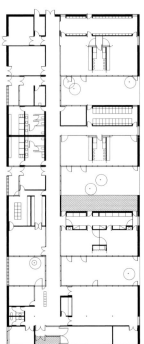

← | Green sloping roof
↓ | Hallway

Dominique Coulon et associés

↑ | Exterior view from garden
↓ | Section and floor plan

Nursery School in Marmoutier

The geometrical simplicity of the building and the widespread use of natural materials reveal this kindergarten's respectful relationship with its environment. Fences are made of dried heather and the grounds are covered in fine sand, while a basin in the middle of the school collects rainwater. All five classrooms benefit from two orientations which allow natural light and ventilation to flow into the rooms. A cell measures the exact quantity of light necessary, thereby eliminating superfluous energy consumption. Aside from the environmental aspects, the spaces themselves are the key concept of the project: they are varied, playful and scaled to the children who use them.

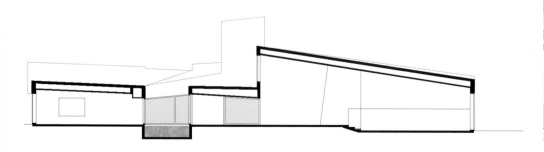

PROJECT FACTS

Location: Mar de Lattre De Tassigny 24, 67440 Marmoutier, France. **Completion year:** 2006. **Group size:** 3 groups. **Educational approach:** Montessori.

↑ | Detail of interior roof planes

↑ | Classroom
↓ | Building incorporated into the landscape

↑ | **Tunnel carved into playground**
↗ | **Playground with extended garden**
→ | **Detail of classroom windows**

Paletten

Like a flower whose seed grains are surrounded by petals, the common room of this day-care center is a central area accessed from the surrounding group rooms. In this way, all functions are closely connected to the common room and to each other, which is extremely practical whilst also manifesting the symbolic importance of community in the spirit and design of the project. Each room is shaped as a hexagon and therefore connected to all others and part of a unified whole. Yet each room is also a different color, allowing the children to address concepts of uniqueness and identity. Materials used for the façades and roof supports further support the key concept of diversity alongside recognition.

PROJECT FACTS

Address: Hoppesvej 25, Vonsild, 6000 Kolding, Denmark. **Completion year:** 2010. **Gross floor area:** 1,200 m².

↑ | Playground with sandbox
← | Activity room
↓ | Hexagon floor plans

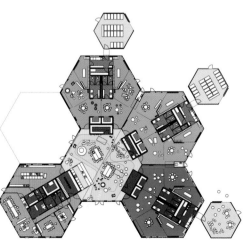

← | Classroom with windows punched at different heights
↓ | Aerial view

VAUMM arquitectura
& urbanismo

↑ | South and south-east view
↗ | Façade detail
→ | Children's scale windows in corridors

Kindergarten and Parking in Sansaburu

Opening towards the south and south-east, Sansaburu Kindergarten is composed of two wings surrounding a central courtyard. Each arm of the building has two stories in which the various elements are organized. The classrooms have been arranged in order to receive the most possible natural light at the times when they are in use. Large windows at ground level allow light to flood into the interior spaces and also create a relationship between interior and exterior. The warm colors that clad the interior extend beyond the internal spaces through a random arrangement of gaps in the façade. An arrangement of lamps in the front entrance above the tramex-made closure draws the gaze of passers-by.

PROJECT FACTS
Address: Calle de Sansaburu 2, 20600 Eibar, Spain. **Completion year:** 2007. **Gross floor area:** 1,227 m².
Group size: 43 children.

↑ | Exterior view by night
← | Classroom

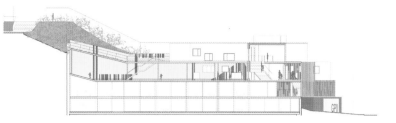

← | Staircase
↑ | Section
↓ | Tramex-made building closure

↑ | **Detail of triangular continuous roof-surfaces**
↗ | **Aerial view**
→ | **Playground**

Bubbletecture M

Shuhei Endo's purpose in the extensive use of wood in this project was to form a new architecture for a new environmental age. The wooden shell's form was dictated by the required sizes of the individual spaces—four classrooms, a playroom, staff room, conference room and playground. Necessarily, the areas which demand the most space, including the playroom, have formed the highest roof. The expansive roof conveys a sense of continuity, while simultaneously maintaining clearly defined spaces, creating an impression of a series of bubbles fused together. Wooden beams and hexagonal steel fittings are combined in various configurations to ensure continually changing and exciting spaces.

PROJECT FACTS　**Address:** Maibara-city, Shiga Prefecture, Japan. **Completion year:** 2003. **Gross floor area:** 1,243 m².

↑ | Detail of shell-form roof extends down
to ground
← | Lobby

← | Interior view of ceiling with wooden
beams and hexagonal fittings
↓ | Elevations

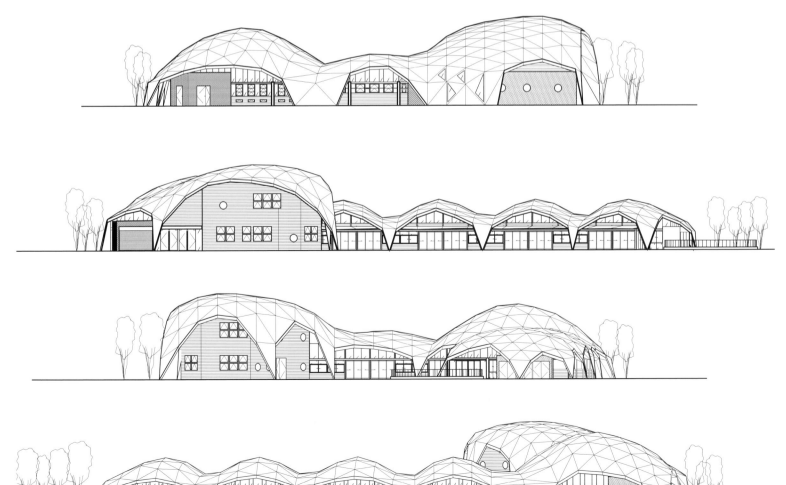

BmasC Architects

↑ | Glass façade reveals colorful interior
↓ | Wooden fence surrounding buildings

↓ | Floor plan

Kindergarten in Sotillo
de la Adrada

A solid perimeter fence, sometimes following the outline of the plot, sometimes seeking the best route over land, separates this new center for pre-school education from the numerous new housing units surrounding the site. Inside the fence, the building is condensed into two closed spaces connected by an arm of light and glass, and two patios. The interior reveals spaces with qualities of color bestowed by the lacquered finish of the aluminium carpentry work and colored ceramic surfaces. The circulation spaces have been designed to allow the children their own visual relationship with the spaces outside. The uppermost limits of the classrooms are marked by hanging lamps.

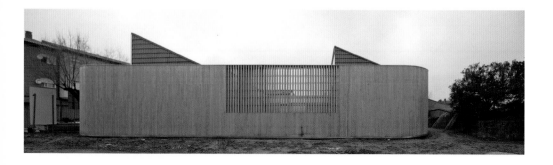

PROJECT FACTS

Address: Martires St., Avila, Spain. **Completion year:** 2007. **Gross floor area:** 1,280 m². **Group size:** 16 children.

↑ | **Inner façade with skylight**

↑ | **Activity room**
↓ | **Courtyard**

Akio Nakasa + Tomohiro
Tanaka / naf
architect & design

↑ | **Building curve encloses trees**
→ | **Stairs with transparent ceiling**

Machida Shizen-Kindergarten

Low-rise buildings are scattered in the vast premises of this kindergarten amongst trees and foliage. Preserving the natural environment was a key concern for the architects. As a result, a cherry tree was left in the middle of Building K and Building L, whose shape forms a gentle curve, was built enclosing trees. Building M, constructed as a corridor to connect buildings and provide shelter from rain, was designed with stairs built half-underground and with transparent walls and ceiling that showcase the landscape. Building E is characterized by full-height, glazed, sliding doors, which are covered in transparent film of various colors at the eye-height of a child.

Address: Tadao, Machida-shi, Tokyo, Japan. **Completion year:** 2008. **Gross floor area:** 1,351 m². **Group size:** 30 children (9 groups).

↑ | **Exterior view**
← | **View from forest**

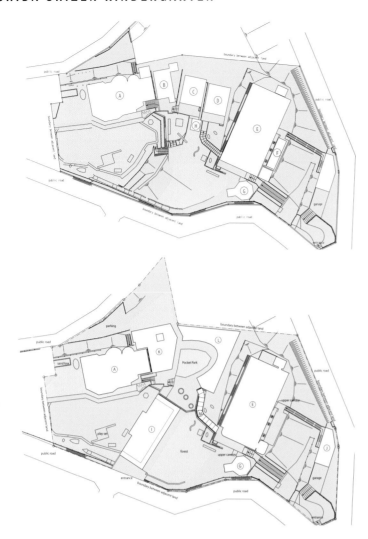

← | Site plans
↓ | Building preserves natural environment

Gálvez + Wieczorek
arquitectura

↑ | Exterior view from playground
→ | Patio with a continuous polycarbonate façade

La Corita Kindergarten

The building flows onto a south-facing courtyard through a façade made of cellular poly-carbonate panels that filter the entry of light. The project aimed to accommodate the natural behavior of children, who spend a lot of time in direct contact with the floor, either lying or sitting, and also looking upwards at the ceiling. A patchwork of different colors covers the floor area to stimulate the children and enable spatial orientation and the ceiling has been drilled with openings that produce colored lights which vary with time. The light filtered through these openings and through the translucent façade create an ideal space for magical or unexpected perceptions.

PROJECT FACTS
Address: Calle de la Libertad 108, 28340 Valdemoro (Madrid), Spain. **Completion year:** 2005. **Gross floor area:** 1,397 m². **Group size:** 8 children per group.

↑ | Yellow ceiling skylights filtering daylight
← | Play house structure in outdoor sand area

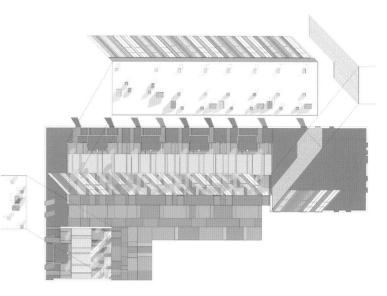

← | Exterior view by night
↑ | Floor plan diagram
↓ | Detail of thick, flat roof and vertical Trespa panels

Frederik, 7 years

Lara, 5 years

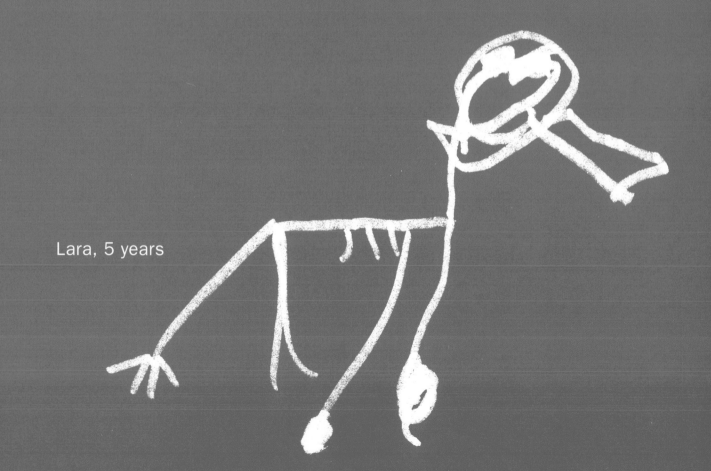

Tosca, 2 years

LARGE
1500+ m²

BP Architectures member of
Collective PLAN 01

↑ | **Playroom with panelled roof**
→ | **View to courtyard**

Epinay Nursery School

The nursery is located on the edge of a 1970s estate characterized by tall, massive and rectangular features. With its bright colors and modern look, this nursery is at odds with the surrounding built context, but entirely in tune with the imaginative world of childhood. The project consists of five entities, all linked to childhood, but each one distinct and requiring its own configuration and access. These small units lie at right angles to the main access road and alternate with strips of vegetation. Each unit has a panelled roof whose slope differs according to the activities underneath. The height to ridge beam and the resulting available internal space are linked to the room's importance.

PROJECT FACTS Address: 3 rue Alsace Lorraine , 91860 Epinay-sur-sénart, France. **Completion year:** 2010. **Gross floor area:** 1,500 m². **Educational approach:** Project-based. **Group size:** 12 children.

↑ | Passage linking different units
← | View to playground from passage
↓ | Floor plan

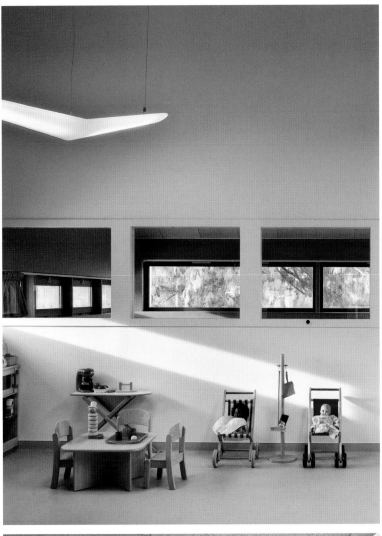

← | Play area
↙ | Classroom
↓ | Aerial view

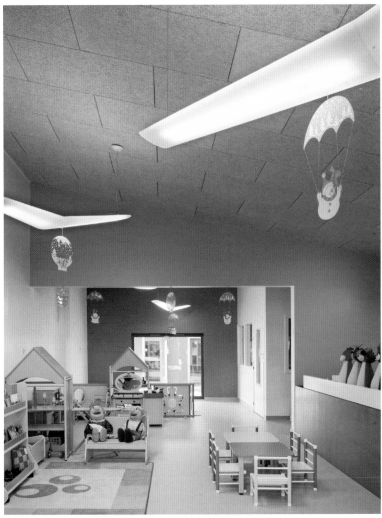

Rudy Uytenhaak
Architectenbureau BV

↑ | Schoolyard at main entrance
→ | Hallway with colorful shelves

Montessori School Landsmeer

Based on the Montessori model of education, in which the classroom forms the home base of a group of pupils but also merges into the greater whole, this school has a corresponding freely adaptable structure with no load-bearing separating walls. The journey to knowledge, or "didactic wandering", is represented in spatial terms by a construction area which forms the connection between the classrooms of the various age groups. A striking and theatrical footbridge at the entrance leads to the first floor where a multifunctional space houses the communal facilities. From this "mezzanine" floor, parents and children can descend to the ground floor, where the schoolyard and classrooms are located.

PROJECT FACTS
Address: Burgemeester Postweg 88, 1121 JC Landsmeer, Netherlands. **Completion year:** 2008. **Gross floor area:** 1,500 m². **Educational approach:** Montessori. **Group size:** 26 children.

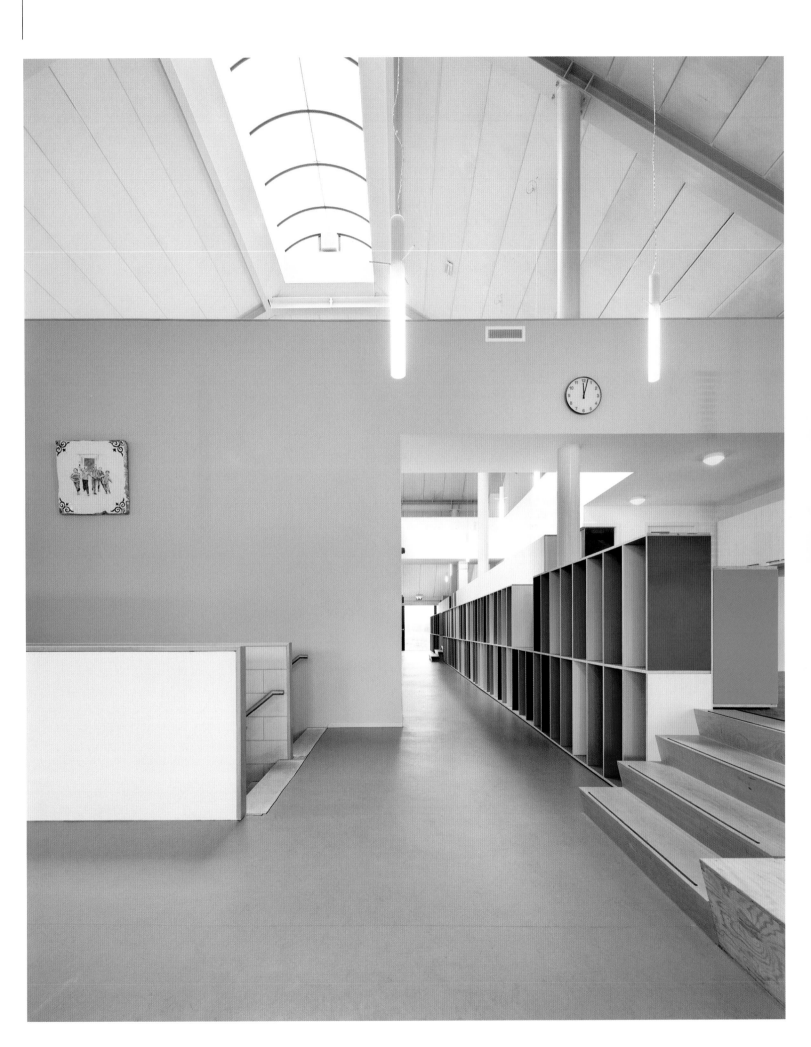

↑ | View to footbridge at entrance
← | Gallery space

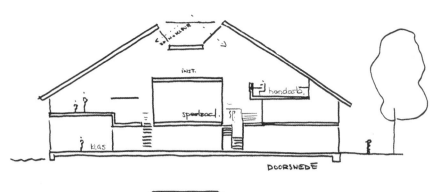

DOORSNEDE

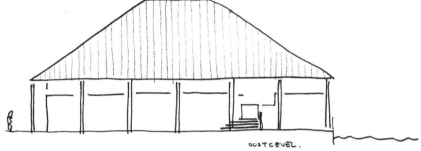

OOSTGEVEL.

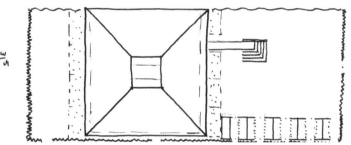

← | Sketches
↓ | Exterior view

Javier Larraz

↑ I **Colorful pendant lamps floating in hallway**
↗ I **Play area**
→ I **Central space connecting the children's areas**

Nursery School in Pamplona

The building is organized as a series of four parallel bodies in which fully built and empty areas are alternated. A body with administration services is located at the west of the site and filters the traffic noise from this side. The empty central space is illuminated through a skylight that emerges above the rest of the building and a third body houses the children's areas, including classrooms, workshops, refectories and bedrooms. Lastly, the external backyard is conceived as a prolongation of the classroom spaces through the opening of large windows. Diverse colors and textures (concrete, rubber and grass) create suggestive and varied playing spaces for the children.

PROJECT FACTS

Address: Parcela E.1.1 - Buztintxuri, 31002 Pamplona, Navarra, Spain. **Completion year:** 2009. **Gross floor area:** 1,519 m². **Building capacity:** 68 children (3 groups).

↑ | **Exterior view**
↙ | **Floor plan**

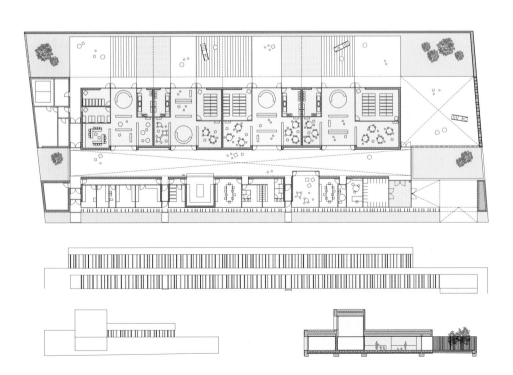

← | Central area with double-height ceilings
↓ | Enclosed outdoor area

↑ | Main entrance
↗ | Front façade
→ | Playground

Las Viñas Infant Educational Center

Located in the northern part of Cullar Vega's city center, the project articulates itself around the idea of creating a permeable building, in which Verd exterior space and its relation with the interior play the leading roles. Two main complementary crossing axes, one enclosing public activities and administration, the other, longer, the teaching activities and classrooms, structure the building. All spaces receive natural light and ventilation and are interconnected in order to achieve visual integration of all inner areas. The perimeter wall is dense to align the school with its urban surroundings, yet also permeable, allowing views of the grounds from beyond the wall.

PROJECT FACTS

Address: Paseo Quijote de la Mancha s/n, 18195 Cúllar Vega, Granada, Spain. **Completion year:** 2009.
Gross floor area: 1,675 m². **Group size:** 20 children.

↑ | **Detail of roof canopy**
← | **Outdoor area**

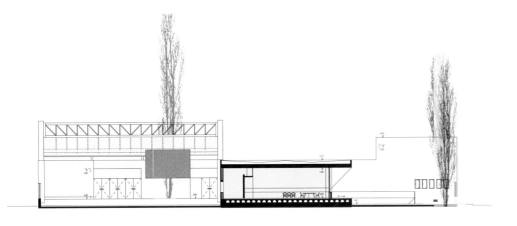

← | Sections
↓ | Courtyard by night

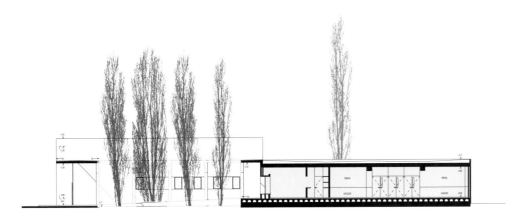

Magén Arquitectos

↑ | Brown classroom
→ | Courtyard

Kindergarten in Rosales del Canal

This project is based closely on children's perception of the constructed environment: Magén Arquitectos wanted to combine the general volumetrics with a domestic scale and the sensory relationship between children and architecture. The classroom forms the basic unit and the roofing style is repeated to cover spaces that occupy a larger surface area such as the multipurpose hall and the dining room. The general configuration of the building responds to clearly organisational criteria, with the classrooms placed around the patio with service spaces situated between them. A combination of horizontal and vertical wooden panels and colored boards forms an apparently adventurous composition.

PROJECT FACTS

Address: Calle de Piotr Ilych Tchaikovsky, 50012 Zaragoza, Spain. **Completion year:** 2009. **Gross floor area:** 1, 720 m². **Group size:** 25 children.

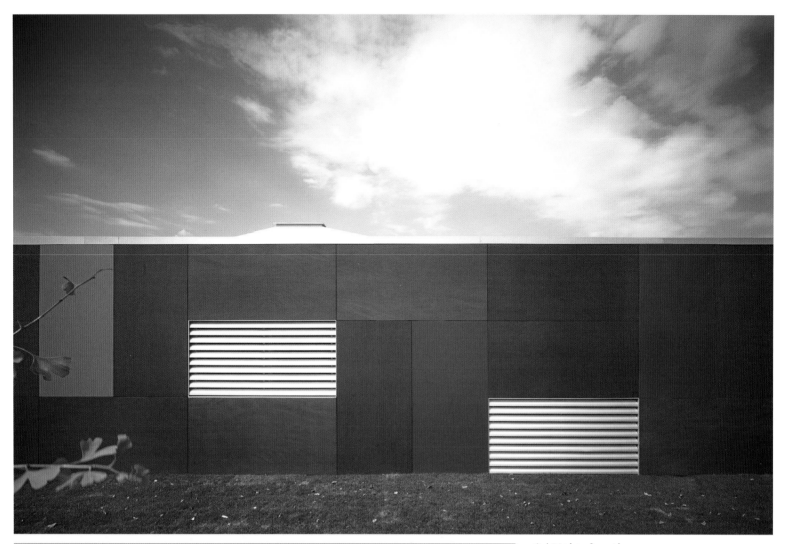

↑ | **Main elevation**
← | **Lobby**

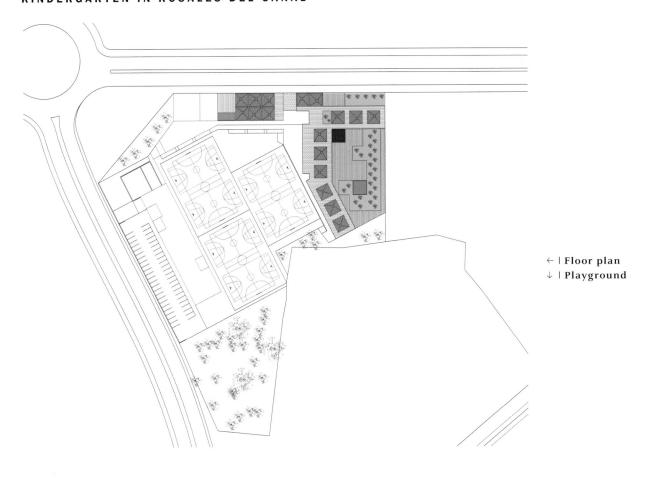

← | **Floor plan**
↓ | **Playground**

Randic Turato architects

↑ | Aerial view
→ | Stonewall façade

Katarina Frankopan Kindergarten

Shaped as an introverted insula and bordered by soaring stone walls, this kindergarten detaches itself from the unattractive surroundings of apartments and shopping malls. Inside, individual units are combined with open gardens and connected with pedestrian walkways. Due to the relatively small area of the site, the units for the smallest children along with open roof terraces are located on the first floor. The kindergarten is defined by a series of halls, or kale (local name for small streets), that are slanted upwards or downwards according to the topography of the site. A small piazza in the center of the kindergarten serves as a location for events and celebrations.

PROJECT FACTS

Address: Krk Island, Croatia. **Completion year:** 2009. **Gross floor area:** 1,725 m². **Building capacity:** 72 children (4 groups).

↑ | **Main entrance**
← | **Lobby**

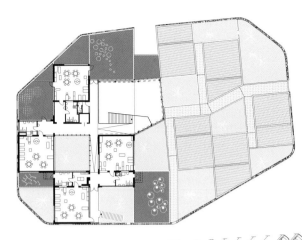

← | Floor plans
↓ | Playroom with view to landscape

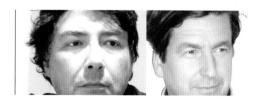

↑ | Exterior view from street
↓ | Floor plans

↘ | Interior sketch

Saint Petri Parish
Hall with Crèche

In keeping with the historical plot foundation, a new community center with day care and pastoral care facilities was erected on the Petrikirche Square. The property surroundings are marked by the church and Hulbe-Haus in the immediate vicinity. The structure is aligned with the adjacent building, orienting in its design to the themes typical for the district. The staggered community center creates rooftop terraces for the sexton's apartment and the vestry, thereby generating a fascinating roof landscape. The outside playground belonging to the day care center is enclosed by a wall which connects the structure with the layout of the square.

PROJECT FACTS   **Address:** Bei der Petrikirche 3, 20095 Hamburg, Germany. **Completion year:** 2009. **Gross floor area:** 1,800 m². **Group size:** 16-24 children per group (4 groups).

↑ | **Front façade**

↓ | **Interior View**

Alberto Campo Baeza

↑ | **Exterior view from surroundings**
↗→ | **Courtyards**

Daycare Center for Benetton

The square box housing this daycare center is composed Caf nine smaller squares, the central one emerging above the rest to allow in extra light. This space recalls a haman in the way sunlight is gathered through perforations in the ceiling and facades. Classrooms are arranged in the surrounding squares. A larger, circular enclosure made up of double circular walls embraces the square structure. Four courtyards, tensed between the curved and straight walls and open to the air, evoke the four elements: air, earth, fire and water. The space between the perimeter walls serves as a "secret place" for the children.

PROJECT FACTS **Address:** Treviso, Italy. **Completion year:** 2008. **Gross floor area:** 1,868 m². **Building capacity:** 100 children.

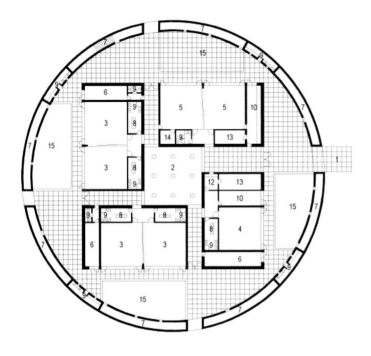

← ← | Vestibule
← | Floor plan
↙ | Exterior view
↓ | Courtyards

witry & witry architecture
urbanisme

↑ | **Exterior view**
↗ | **Detail façade**
→ | **Plantation on the 1st floor**

Children's Day Nursery
and Pre-School Hamm

The two-story nursery and pre-school was constructed of timber frames as a low energy building. The upper floor contains plant rooms, in which the children can harvest plants from a variety of continents including coffee, urbanas and pineapples. A covered recreation hall is open over both floors and has an energy regulating effect: the special planting has a positive impact on air quality and micro climate. An information board in the hall displays the current supply of energy produced by the photovoltaic elements on the roof. The constant visibility of the energy values aims to raise the awareness of the children to the issue of renewable energy.

PROJECT FACTS

Address: 159 Rue de Hamm, 1713 Luxembourg District, Luxembourg. **Completion year:** 2008. **Gross floor area:** 2,014 m².

↑ | **Foyer**
← | **Interior planting**

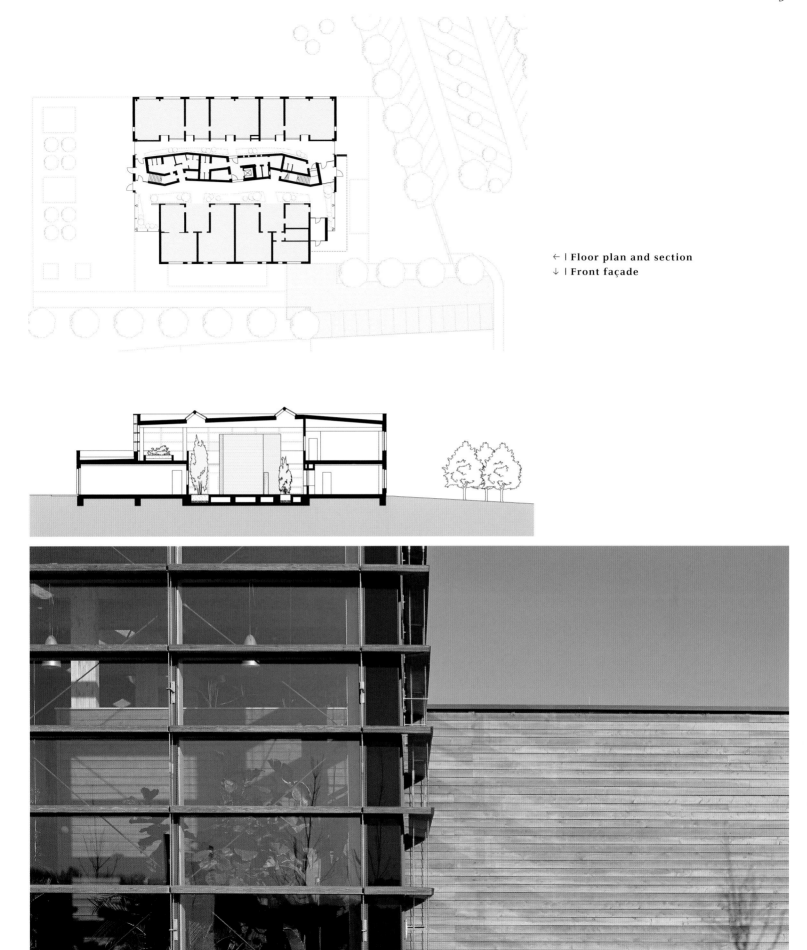

← | Floor plan and section
↓ | Front façade

↑ | **Playground and exterior view**
↓ | **Floorplan and section**

Daycare Center
Josefinum

Drawing on the theme of Noah's ark, the new building was conceived as a ship docked on the embankment of the Mur. The access leads to a covered open space which connects the school grounds with the day nursery and the kindergarten. On the river side the building is two stories high, with the kindergarten on the ground floor. The day nursery groups are located in the upper floor, the balcony of which extends like a railing along the entire building grounds to the terrace, which like a ship's deck, offers yet more open space. On the schoolyard side the structure is one story in height and organized into four separate structures by means of atriums. All group rooms orient to the garden, so that the facility can be operated without disruption.

PROJECT FACTS

Address: Erzherzog Johannstraße 1, 8700 Leoben, Austria. **Completion year:** 2009. **Gross floor area:** 2,180 m². **Group size:** 20 children (5 groups).

↑ | Wooden balcony

↑ | Exterior staircase leading to classrooms
↓ | View to playground

↑ | **Covered winter terraces**
↗ | **Exterior side view**
→ | **Interior courtyard**

Kindergarten MB

Kindergarten MB was conceived as a single-story mat building - compact and introverted with clearly defined borders - as a response to the challenges of the site, which is overshadowed by a nine-story block to the south and surrounded by heavy traffic. A repetitive small-scale structure of units and patios echoes the local suburban matrix and creates a variety of open-air spaces, including covered (winter) terraces and a roof-top garden. The interior is organized as a sequence of spaces linked with "The Children's Street". Its meandering character and multitude of in-between spaces, supported by transparency and color coding, create a scenery of true "urban" experience for the child.

PROJECT FACTS
Address: Ulica Dubrava, Zagreb, Croatia. **Completion year:** 2008. **Gross floor area:** 2,300 m². **Group size:** 20 children (2 groups).

↑ | **Street view**
← | **Classroom**
↓ | **Floor plan**

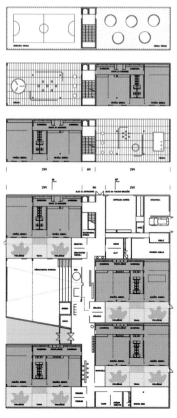

← | Playground
↓ | Interior with transparent glass walls

Bureau Bos

↑ | **Front façade**
↓ | **Floor plans**

De Uitkijck

This center for education and childcare houses a primary school and two organisations for baby- and childcare. The building is planned around an open central space used by all parties and containing a yellow, cone-shaped volume with the libary and a small theater / stage. Organized by age, the building houses the younger children on the ground floor and the older children on the first floor with its French balcony. A sloping roof gradually rises from one to two-and-a-half stories, creating more space in some sub-level floors and a dry main entrance. Both inside and outside, wide stairs lead from the ground floor to the first floor. These stairs are also used as galleries during events.

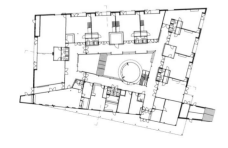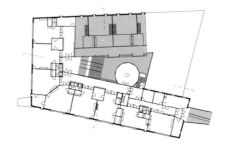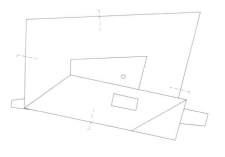

PROJECT FACTS
Address: Margrietstraat 2, 3742 RC Baarn, Netherlands. **Completion year:** 2009. **Gross floor area:** 2,375 m². **Educational approach:** Dalton. **Group size:** 23 children.

↑ | Lobby

↑ | Main entrance
↓ | Side view

Penezic & Rogina Architects

↑ | Façade with colored Trespa plates
→ | Staircase leading to playground

Kindergarten and Nursery Jarun

Space is provided for ten educational groups in this kindergarten and nursery, which combines optimal functionality, accessibility, transparency rond openness in its linear structure. Three interconnected units comprise the interior: the nursery on the ground floor, the kindergarten units on both the ground and first floors and the service rooms organised around a housekeeping yard. The units can be completely opened onto sheltered terraces or deep canopied balconies on warm days, spaces which also serve to activate the linear volume and decode the function of the interior spaces. Materials such as aluminium, glass, linoleum and colored Trespa plates further emphasize the main features.

PROJECT FACTS **Address:** Bartolici 39a, Zagreb, Croatia. **Completion year:** 2006. **Gross floor area:** 2,570 m². **Group size:** 20 children (3 nursery and 7 kindergarten groups).

↑ | Playground
← | Detail of buildig volume
↓ | Floor plans

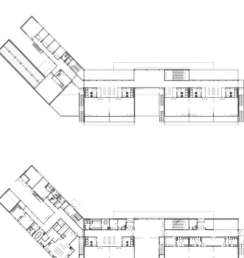

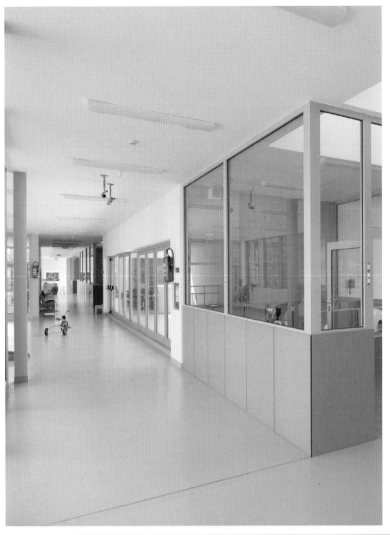

← | Hallway
↓ | Exterior front view

Jarmund/Vigsnæs AS
Architects MNAL

↑ | Outdoor area
→ | Exterior view during winter

Oslo International School

The existing 1960s structure was worn down but had obvious architectonic qualities which the architects aimed to preserve, including organization on one level enabling easy orientation, good natural lighting and close contact to the outdoors. A pavilion separate from the rest of the school houses the smallest children in ten classooms. The room sizes are flexible and can be altered according to the number of children on each level. Daylight from the atrium floods the common areas. The organically shaped walls are clad with specially milled wooden paneling in convex and concave shape, treated with clear tar and the façade is covered with fiber cement boards in ten different colors.

Address: Gamle Ringeriksvei 53, 1357 Bekkestua, Norway. Landscape Architect: Grindaker AS.
Completion year: 2009. Gross floor area: 3,300 m². Group size: 20 children (2 groups).

↑ | **Main entrance**
← | **Diagrammatic floor plans**

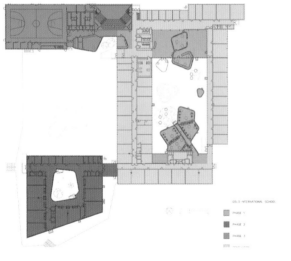

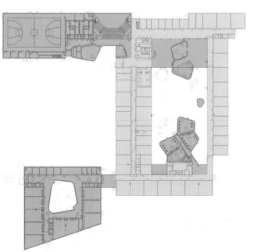

← | Hallway with filtered light
↓ | General view

↑ | **Chapel**
↓ | **Elevation and floor plan**

Copalita School and Civic Center

Part of a community project to relocate a town destroyed by flooding, the school was planned around an existing natural garden in a key location on the new site and played a key role in developing an identity for the town. Existing trees have been enclosed by the school buildings to create recreational patios as spaces for education and play. The project orchestrates a low cost technology solution to cope with the hot climate, combining natural light and ventilation, eliminating the use of glass in the windows and using heavy earth walls and ceramic lattice as a cross ventilation atmosphere solution. The new public space unites the school with a new open chapel.

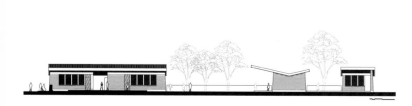

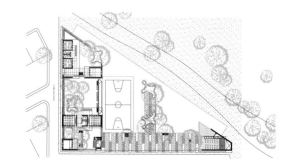

PROJECT FACTS

Address: Copalita, Huatulco, Oaxaca, Mexico. **Completion year:** 2009. **Gross floor area:** 4,300 m².
Educational approach: Montessori. **Group size:** 10 children per group.

↑ | View from main portico

↑ | Playground
↓ | View from kindergarten to the primary school

Rudy Uytenhaak
Architectenbureau BV

↑ | Exterior view by night
↓ | Elevations

Multi Functional Center Leeuwarden

Two elementary schools, a community center for young and old, a crèche and a sports hall are combined in a compact and dynamic building. The building functions as a "guiding light" for the whole neighborhood: literally through its transparent façade and more figuratively through the functions it accommodates. The different user groups are organized within the building in such a way that they can use it autonomously, each with their own entrance, so preserving their identity. It is also possible to link or exchange the spaces for the various user groups. The building is heated and cooled with the use of concrete core activation in combination with a heat pump.

PROJECT FACTS

Address: Droppingsstraat 14, 8923 BW Leeuwarden, Netherlands. **Completion year:** 2009. **Gross floor area:** 4,300 m². **Group size:** 15 children.

↑ | Schoolyard

↑ | Wooden staircase
↓ | View to transparent building envelope

↑ | **Exterior side view**
→ | **Façade detail**

Forum 't Zand

Forum 't Zand is an extended school adjacent to an archaeological park with Roman ruins and surrounded by the remains of a recent horticultural past. In order to leave the valuable grounds and the surrounding nature as untouched as possible, a compact design was chosen which provides for multiple use of land and rooms. A number of playgrounds were situated on the roof, providing a saving in land costs and, in addition, obviating the need for fencing. As a result the school grounds became the extension of an adjacent park. Surrounded by the remnants of earlier civilisations, this science fiction spacecraft adds a new layer to history and offers an appealing cultural centre for the neighborhood.

PROJECT FACTS

Address: Pauwoogvlinder 12-24, Leidsche Rijn, Utrecht, The Netherlands. **Landscape architects:** OKRA landscape architects. **Completion year:** 2005. **Gross floor area:** 7,100 m². **Educational approach:** Montessori. **Group size:** 30 children (10 groups).

↑ | View to sportshall
← | Hallway

← | Foyer
↓ | Exterior view

↑ | **Exterior view**
↓ | **Sections**

Primary School Daycare Center and Sports Hall

The Primary School Day Care Center and Sports Hall in the Frankfurt district of Riedberg is one of the first passive house schools in Germany. Thanks to the passive house standards, not only are the operating costs of the school and the day care reduced—the heating energy savings amount to 90 percent, the room climate is also noticeably improved, providing an exceptional amenity value. In addition the flexible area, with an exercise and relaxation space, workshop, construction and theater space as well as the expansive grounds, offers the children many activity opportunities and enough play area for their various needs for movement, creativity or relaxation.

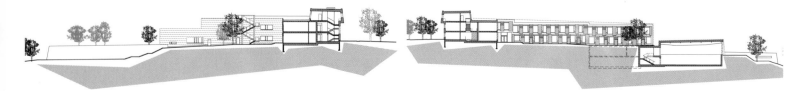

PROJECT FACTS | **Address:** Zur Kalbacher Höhe 15, 60439 Frankfurt am Main / Riedberg. **Completion year:** 2004. **Gross floor area:** 8,785 m². **Group size:** 10 children (5 groups).

257

↑ | **View to garden**
↓ | **Detail façade**

↑ | Atrium and dining area
→ | Theater

Dietro la Vigna

Meaning "behind the vineyard", this nursery follows certain features of the existing site to amplify its peculiarity and unique qualities. The main hall, where most of the learning activities take place, faces the vineyard, offering a unique opportunity for the children to be in constant contact with the landscape, and receives a substantial amount of soft light from the north. All internal spaces follow the concepts of promoting learning and stimulating the sensorial experience of architecture, whether a broad or a narrow room, a high or low ceiling, a dynamic or fixed space. In each space, pedagogical concepts cohere with architectonic solutions to determine the children's behavior and awareness.

↑ | **Play area Dining area**
← | **Play area**

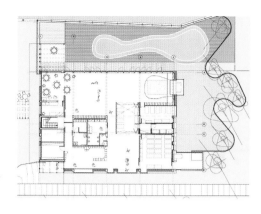

← | View from second floor
↑ | Floor plan
↓ | North front, overlooking vineyards

Index

Arch

itects Index

128 Architecture & Urban Design

Salvador Alvarado 128A-3 Col. Escandon
Mexico City 11800 (Mexico)
T +52 55 52724610
www.128asc.com

→ 248

4a Architekten

Hallstrasse 25
70376 Stuttgart (Germany)
T +49 711 38930000
F +49 711 389300099
kontakt@4a-architekten.de
www.4a-architekten.de

→ 256

70°N Arkitektur

Strandvegen 144, P.B 1247
9262 Tromso (Norway)
T +47 77 662670
F +47 77 662679
firmapost@70n.no
www.70n.no

→ 52

Aeby & Perneger

rue de Veyrier 19
1227 Carouge (Switzerland)
T +41 22 8096666
F + 41 22 8096667
mail@aeby-perneger.ch
www.aeby-perneger.ch

→ 126

AFKS Architects

Ratakatu 19
00120 Helsinki (Finland)
T +358 9 2788788
F +358 9 2788798
afks@afks.fi
www.afks.fi

→ 122

(BP) Architectures member of Collective PLAN 01

89 rue de Reuilly
75012 Paris (France)
T +33 1 53332420
F +33 1 53332421
agencebp@agencebp.com
www.agencebp.com

→ 198

Akyol Kamps Architekten

Shaarsteinbergbrücke 2
20459 Hamburg (Germany)
T +49 40 22622640
F +49 40 226226410
office@akyol-kamps.de
www.akyol-kamps.de

→ 222

Bernardo Bader

Steinebach 11
6850 Dornbirn (Austria)
T +43 557 2207896
F +43 557 2207896
mail@bernardobader.com
www.bernardobader.com

→ 68

Béal & Blanckaert architectes associés

Steinebach 11
6850 Dornbirn (Austria)
T +43 557 2207896
F +43 557 2207896
mail@bernardobader.com
www.bernardobader.com

→ 88, 134

BmasC Architects

c/ Caballeros, 19. 2º Izda.
05001 Ávila (Spain)
T +34 920 250669
estudio@bmasc.es
www.bmasc.es

→ 186

Agence Beckmann-N'Thépé Architectes

5 rue d'Hauteville
75010 Paris (France)
T +33 1 48244840
F +33 1 48240209
info@b-nt.biz
www.b-nt.biz

→ 20

Pietro Boschetti

Via Castausio 5
6900 Lugano (Switzerland)
T +41 91 9232354
F +41 91 9232384
info@pietroboschetti.ch
www.pietroboschetti.ch

→ 48

Brendeland & Kristoffersen

Fjordgata 50
7010 Trondheim (Norway)
T +47 73 536210
firma@bkark.no
www.bkark.no

→ 36

Bureau Bos

Postbus 636
3740 AP Baarn (The Netherlands)
T +31 35 5416342
F +31 35 5413582
www.bureaubos.nl

→ 238

Bonnard Woeffray Architectes

Clos-Donroux 1
1870 Monthey (Switzerland)
T +41 24 4722970
F +41 24 4722971
bw@bwarch.ch
bwarch.ch

→ 164

Estudio Arquitectura Campo Baeza

Almirante 9, 2 izq
28004 Madrid (Spain)
T +34 917 010695
F +34 915 217061
estudio@campobaeza.com
www.campobaeza.com

→ 224

ccd studio

Corso Cerulli 1
64100 Teramo (Italy)
T +39 861 250 993
F +39 861 252 901
grafica@ccdstudio.eu
www.ccdstudio.eu

→ 154

CEBRA

Vesterbro Torv 1-3. 2. SAL
8000 Aarhus C (Denmark)
T +45 8730 3439
F +45 8730 3429
cebra@cebra.info
www.cebra.info

→ 174

cercadelcielo. studio architecture

Plaza Federico Servet 4, 2D
30003 Murcia (Spain)
co.estudio@coamu.es
www.cercadelcielo.es

→ 16

C. F. Møller Architects

Europaplads 2, 11
8000 Århus C (Denmark)
T +45 8730 5300
cfmoller@cfmoller.com
www.cfmoller.com

→ 142

Antonio Citterio Patricia Viel and Partners

Via Cerva 4
20122 Milan (Italy)
T +39 02 7638801
F +39 02 76388080
info@antoniocitterioandpartners.it
www.antoniocitterioandpartners.it

→ 56

Dominique Coulon et associés

5 quai de Paris
67000 Strasbourg (France)
T +33 3 88321761
F +33 3 88322643
agence@coulon-architecte.fr
www.coulon-architecte.fr

→ 172

C + S Associati

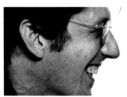

Piazza San Leonardo 15
31100 Treviso (Italy)
T +39 04 22591796
press@cipiuesse.it
www.cipiuesse.it

→ 90

De8 architetti

via Portico 59/61
24050 Orio al Serio, Bergamo (Italy)
T +39 03 5530050
F +39 03 5533725
info@deottostudio.com
www.deottostudio.com

→ 258

Dietrich Untertrifaller Architekten

Arlbergstrasse 117
6900 Bregenz (Austria)
T +43 557 4788880
F +43 557 47888820
arch@dietrich.untertrifaller.com
www.dietrich.untertrifaller.com

→ 146

D'Inka Scheible Hoffmann Architekten BDA

Kelterweg 20
70734 Fellbach (Germany)
T +49 711 25859950
F +49 711 258599529
info@dinkascheiblehoffmann.de
www.dinkascheiblehoffmann.de

→ 108

Dorte Mandrup Arkitekter

Nørrebrogade 66D, 1.SAL
DK-2200 Copenhagen (Denmark)
T +45 3393 7350
info@dortemandrup.dk
www.dortemandrup.dk

→ 116

Drost + van Veen architecten

Dunantstraat 4
3024 BC Rotterdam (The Netherlands)
T +31 10 4774964
F +31 10 4776259
architecten@drostvanveen.nl
www.drostvanveen.nl

→ 40

Ecker Architekten

Iglauer Straße 13
74722 Buchen im Odenwald (Germany)
T +49 6281 565654
F +49 6281 563570
ecker@ecker-architekten.de
www.ecker-architekten.de

→ 60

Shuhei Endo

F2-14-5, Tenma, Kita-ku, Osaka
530-0043 (Japan)
T +81 06 63547456
F +81 06 63547457
endo@paramodern.com
www.paramodern.com

→ 182

Hans Finner Architekt + Carroquino Arquitectos

Hütten 49
20355 Hamburg (Germany)
T +49 40 21055990
F +49 32 121108068
mail@hansfinner.de
www.hansfinner.de

→ 168

Gabu Heindl Architektur

Schottenfeldgasse 72/VI-b
1070 Vienna (Austria)
T +43 676 3643387
arc.gabuheindl@gmx.at
www.gabu-wang.at

→ 32

Gálvez + Wieczorek arquitectura

c/ Leganitos 1, 1 dcha.
28013 Madrid (Spain)
T +34 915 421046
www.galvez-wieczorek.com

→ 192

Hamonic + Masson

93 rue Montmartre
75002 Paris (France)
T +33 1 53 629943
F +33 1 53 629938
contact@hamonic-masson.com
www.hamonic-masson.com

→ 150

Susanne Hofmann Architekten. Baupiloten

Straße des 17. Juni 152
10623 Berlin (Germany)
T +49 30 31428923
F +49 30 314.28925
post@baupiloten.com
www.baupiloten.com

→ 44

Jarmund/Vigsnæs AS Architects MNAL

Hausmanngate 6
0186 Oslo (Norway)
T +47 2299 4343
jva@jva.no
www.jva.no

→ 244

Kadawittfeldarchitektur

Aureliusstraße 2
52064 Aachen (Germany)
T +49 24 194690
F +49 24 19469020
office@kwa.ac
www.kadawittfeldarchitektur.de

→ 100

Marcio Kogan

Alameda Tietê 505
01417-020 São Paolo (Brazil)
T +55 11 30813522
info@marciokogan.com.br
www.marciokogan.com.br

→ 84

Javier Larraz

c/ Yanguas y Miranda, 1 - 7º
31002 Pamplona, Navarra (Spain)
T +34 948 222483
F +34 948 222483
info@larrazarquitectos.com
www.bergeraphoto.com

→ 206

Lev-Gargir Architects

19 Brodetski st.
69051 Tel Aviv (Israel)
T +972 3 6420523
F +972 3 6420524
www.lev-gargir.com

→ 104

Magén Arquitectos

Paseo Sagasta 54, 7°C
50006 Zaragoza (Spain)
T +34 976 385 110
F +34 976 371 495
estudio@magenarquitectos.com
www.magenarquitectos.com

→ 214

MPH architectes

rue Pré-du-Marché
1004 Lausane (Switzerland)
T +41 21 6463320
info@mpharchitectes.ch
www.ateliermph.ch

→ 120

Akio Nakasa + Tomihiro Tanaka / naf architect & design

8-12-203, Nishihiratsuka-cho, Hiroshima
730-0024 (Japan)
T +81 82 543 4602
F +81 82 543 460
info@naf-aad.com
www.naf-aad.com

→ **188**

Njiric + Arhitekti

Petrova 140
10 000 Zagreb (Croatia)
T +385 1 2335551
F +385 1 2325509
info@njiric.com
www.njiric.com

→ **234**

Nussmüller Architekten

Zinzendorfgasse 1
8010 Graz (Austria)
T +43 316 381812
buero@nussmueller.at
www.nussmueller.at

→ **232**

Taku Sakaushi + Chika Kijima / O.F.D.A.

14 Araki-tyo, Shinjuku-ku
160-0007 Tokyo (Japan)
T +81 3 3358 4303
F +81 3 3358 4304
sakaushi@ofda.jp
www.ofda.jp

→ **72**

Penezic & Rogina Architects

Antuna Bauera 8
10 000 Zagreb (Croatia)
T +385 1 3906331
info@penezic-rogina.com
www.penezic-rogina.com

→ **240**

Randic Turato architects

Delta 5, HR
51000 Rijeka (Croatia)
T +385 51 215456
F +385 51 324650
info@randic-turato.hr
www.randic-turato.hr

→ **218**

raumhochrosen

Bregenzer Straße 47
6900 Bregenz (Austria)
T +43 557 422505
F +43 557 4225054
mail@raumhochrosen.com
www.raumhochrosen.com

→ **28**

RCR Aranda Pigem Vilalta arquitectes

Fontanella 26
17800 Olot, Girona (Spain)
T +34 972 269105
F +34 972 267558
rcr@rcrarquitectes.es
www.rcrarquitectes.es

→ **94**

Architekturbüro Reinberg

Lindengasse 39/10
1070 Vienna (Austria)
T +43 152 48280
F +43 152 4828015
architekt@reinberg.net
www.reinberg.net

→ **80, 158**

Schneider & Lengauer Architekten

Bindergasse 5a
4212 Neumarkt im Mühlkreis (Austria)
T +43 794 189220
F +43 794 189224
office@schneider-lengauer.at
www.schneider-lengauer.at

→ **130**

Solinas Verd Arquitectos

Avenida San Francisco Javier 9
41018 Sevilla (Spain)
T +34 954 926464
F +34 954 926464
solinas-verd@svarquitectos.com
www.svarquitectos.com

→ **210**

Stifter + Bachmann

Bachla 5
39030 Pfalzen Bolzano (Italy)
T +39 04 74529025
F +39 04 74529025
info@stifter-bachmann.com
www.stifter-bachmann.com

→ **76**

studio3 - Institute for Experimental Architecture

Technikerstraße 13
6020 Innsbruck (Austria)
T +43 512 5076651
F +43 512 5072790
studio3@uibk.ac.at
www.olifantsvlei.net

→ **12**

Takahuru+Yui Tezuka Architects

1-19-9-3F Todoroki Setagaya, Tokyo
158-0082 (Japan)
T +81 3 37037056
F +81 3 37037038
tez@sepia.ocn.ne.jp
www.tezuka-arch.com

→ **138**

Rudy Uytenhaak Architectenbureau BV

Schipluidenlaan 4
1062 HE Amsterdam (The Netherlands)
T +31 20 3057777
F +31 20 3057778
arch@uytenhaak.nl
www.uytenhaak.nl

→ **202, 250**

Elisa Valero Ramos

Placeta de San Gil, 10 ático
18010 Granada (Spain)
T +34 95 8223873
info@elisavalero.com
www.elisavalero.com

→ **64**

VAUMM arquitectura&urbanismo

Cuesta de Aldapeta 32
20009 San Sebastián (Spain)
T +34 943 450625
F +34 943 473932
info@vaumm.com
www.vaumm.com

→ **178**

VenhoevenCS

Hoogte Kadijk 143 FIH
1018 BH Amsterdam (The Netherlands)
T +31 20 6228210
F +31 20 6236478
info@venhoevencs.nl
www.venhoevencs.nl

→ **252**

Johannes Wiesflecker

Müllerstraße 10
6020 Innsbruck (Austria)
T +43 512 581551
F +43 512 5815515
office@wiesflecker-architekten.com
www.wiesflecker-architekten.com

→ **160**

witry & witry architecture urbanisme

rue du Pont 32
6471 Echternach (Luxembourg)
T +352 72 88571
F +352 72 88 5799
mail@witry-witry.lu
www.witry-witry.lu

→ **228**

XVStudio

c/ Roger de Flor, 216 Ppal 1a
08013 Barcelona (Spain)
T +34 93 1657314
F +34 93 1620892
info@xvstudio.com
www.xvstudio.com

→ **24**

PICTURE CREDITS

Abadie, Hervé	150
Alda, Fernando	64
Anguera, Jordi	24
Bereuter, Adolf	68, 168
Bergera, Iñaki	206
Bitter, Jan	44
Blanc, Emmanuelle	(127 a.)
Blaževic, Domagoj	234
Boegly, Luc	196
Brodey, Ivan	52, 244
Bstieler, Markus	160
Cappai, Carlo	90
Chemollo, Alessandra	90
Coulon, Gilles	20
Courtesy of bureau bos architecten +	
ingenieurs + adviseurs	238
Courtesy of Nussmüller Architekten	232
Courtesy of Penezic & Rogina Architects	240
Courtesy of RCR Aranda Pigem Vilalta arquitectes	94
Courtesy of studio3	12
de Genève, Ville	120
de Guzmán, Miguel	186, 192
Delonti, Daniele	258
Dragomir, Cosmin	210
Duplan, Jean Pierre	88
Feinen, Michel	228
FOTOTECA/Katsuhisa Kida	138
Frahm, Klaus	222
Frutos, David	16
Garon, Amit	104
Granada, Jesús	214
Grandchamp, Alain	120
Grandorge, David	36
Gutierrez, Alejandro	248
Hart, Rob 't	40
Henz, Hannes	164
Hörbst, Kurt	130
Jantscher, Thomas	126
Johanse, Uffe	142
Kandzia, Christian	256
Kaunat, Angelo	98
Kers, Pieter	202, 250
Klomfar, Bruno	28 146
Kon, Nelson	84
Kramer, Luuk	252
Lauridsen, Per & CEBRA	174
Lendler, Sandro	218
Lindhe, Jens Markus	116
Mantovan, Fabio	154
Matsumura, Yoshiharu	182
Meyer, Constantin	56
Monthiers, Jean-Marie	172
Ortiz, Aitor	178
Otake, Seiichiro	188
Rastl, Lisa	32
Reisch, Michael	112
Schaller, Lukas	76
Scheible, A.	108
Simonetti, Filippo	48
Steiner, Rupert	80, 158
Suzuki, Hisao	224
Tiainen, Jussi	122
Torri, Leo	60
Ueda, Hiroshi	72
Verney, Bertrand	134
Zanta, Marco	224

All other pictures were made available by the architects.

Cover front: Hannes Henz
Cover back left: Bruno Klomfar
right: Nelson Kon

IMPRINT

The Deutsche Bibliothek lists this publication in
the Deutsche Nationalbibliographie; detailed biblio-
graphical information can be found on the Internet at
http://dnb.ddb.de

ISBN 978-3-03768-049-0

© 2011 by Braun Publishing AG
www.braun-publishing.ch

1st edition 2011

Selection of projects and layout: Michelle Galindo
Project coordination and
English text editing: Judith Vonberg
Graphic concept: ON Grafik | Tom Wibberenz
Reproduction: Bild1Druck GmbH, Berlin